Future for All
A vision for 2048

Just · Ecological · Achievable

—

Editorial

–

Authors:

Kai Kuhnhenn, Anne Pinnow, Matthias Schmelzer, Nina Treu

Layout and Cover art:

Diana Neumerkel

Illustrations:

Manuel Schroeder

Translation:

Simon Phillips

Editing and Proofreading:

Andrea Vetter, Eva Mahnke, Josefa Kny, Emily Pickerill, Divij Kapur

Publisher:

Mayfly books

Publishing date:

digital June 2024

printed June 2024

ISBN (Print) 978-1-906948-74-0

ISBN (PDF)   978-1-906948-75-7

Future for All
A vision for 2048

Just · Ecological · Achievable

—

Contents

Imagine waking up
in the year 2048.

Where are you? What is this place like?
What forms of transport do you use?
What sort of foods do you eat?
What do you do during the day?
And how do you participate in society?
If you could leave your current lifestyle
behind for a moment and imagine your
future, what would that future be like?
How can it be just, ecological and
achievable – for everyone?

Bon Voyage

What type of society would you like to live in?
And what can we do to create that society? — *04*

The values behind our vision — *06*

Why do we need a future for all? — *08*

HOW DO WE WANT TO LIVE IN 2048?

▶ 1 Global Justice — *11*

▶ 2 Democracy — *15*

▶ 3 Economy — *20*

▶ 4 Social Security — *25*

▶ 5 Manufacturing and Companies — *29*

▶ 6 Employment — *33*

▶ 7 Technology — *39*

▶ 8 Health and Participation — *45*

▶ 9 Freedom of Movement — *49*

▶ 10 Food and Agriculture — *53*

▶ 11 Housing — *59*

▶ 12 Mobility and Transport — *65*

▶ 13 Energy and Climate — *71*

▶ 14 Education — *75*

▶ 15 Finance — *80*

AND HOW DO WE GET THERE?

The transformation — *86*

How did this vision come about? — *100*

Acknowledgements — *103*

HOW IS THIS BOOK ORGANISED?

→ The first chapter sets out the **basics of our vision** – that is, the values forming the foundation of our vision of the future and the challenges we see in the present.

→ This is followed by chapters describing our vision of society in 2048. Chapters 1 to 7 explain the foundations of the future economy and society, whereas chapters 8 to 16 each focus on one specific area of society.

The chapters include various elements, such as:

Stories, experiences, and letters

written from the point of view of the future.

EXPLANATIONS AND DISCUSSIONS OF CHALLENGES AND CONTENTIOUS ISSUES

written from the point of view of the present.

2024

EXAMPLES

of groups that are already working towards a future for all today

→ The chapter on transformation describes one way in which today's society could develop into a future for all by 2048..

How do we want to live?

It can be difficult to imagine a positive future because our views are peppered with the problems of today's society – the most prominent of which are social and global injustices, environmental destruction and an unequal distribution of power. Yet there is nothing inevitable about how we live today: our society is not a pure reflection of human nature, and we certainly are not destined to live the way we do.

The following vision of society in 2048 is an attempt to free ourselves from the apathy of this supposed lack of alternatives. We aimed to draw up an achievable positive vision that transcends the confines of a capitalist and growth-dependent society. In creating this vision, **we are writing a new chapter in history and describing a future that we are yet to experience**. A vision of a new society was necessary even before the COVID-19 pandemic, the wars in Ukraine and Gaza, and inflation leading to food and energy crises around the world – but it is even more important now. We need ideas that imbue global citizens with encouragement and hope, ideas that make us look forward to the future and inspire us to shape it.

It is no surprise that our ideas have struck a chord, given that so many people today are working towards a just future. Questions about the alternatives to the current economic and social system crop up regularly in projects, social and political groups and initiatives. However, most approaches are focused on the local level, involve narrow policy proposals or simply reflect specific ideological currents. Comprehensive approaches are rarely found. While not intended as a blueprint for a new society, we hope that our vision will inspire people and encourage political debate while also helping to counter nationalist and right-wing populist narratives.

Future for All is the result of a collective writing and networking process. Most of the people involved in developing and discussing the vision are from German-speaking countries. Because the structures and developments in these countries are similar to those found in many other countries in the Global North, our vision should also be applicable to these countries. It is a decolonial vision that aims to change power structures worldwide, but it still stems from an early industrialized, colonizer country. Therefore, it is interwoven with visions and approaches from around the world, but it cannot be applied everywhere because different countries face different problems. Moreover, in many places, people have been discussing and implementing their own approaches to social, environmental and democratic society for a long time.

To paraphrase the Zapatistas, our vision is that of a world into which many worlds fit.

To develop a wide-ranging perspective, we had to **question and partially overcome central aspects of the current economic and social system in the Global North**. Therefore, markets, money, labor and property take on a vastly different role in our vision of the future than they do today. As our daily lives are intertwined with the political framework, transformations of these political systems would also lead to a fundamental change in human relations and our daily lives: how we relate to each other, how we work, love, eat, travel, discuss, make decisions, and how and where we live would change.

Our vision of society in 2048 is neither a prediction of what is to come nor a master plan. Rather, it is one of numerous proposals aimed at understanding the type of society in which people would like to live in as well as the paths that we could take to create such a society. It is unrealistic to assume that the developments outlined below will occur exactly as we describe them. Therefore, **Future for All is an invitation to think, dream, debate and critique**. We hope that *Future for All* will contribute to a broad-based and serious debate about a just and ecological future.

At the time of writing the German editorial (May 2022), the COVID-19 pandemic had caused enormous restrictions to be imposed on public life, and, in turn, created a slowdown in the worldwide economy. As has been the case with the other "crises" that have occurred over the last few decades, the COVID-19 pandemic underscored the inherent structural problems and irrationality of the current system: thousands of people lost their jobs, while important tasks remained undone; climate-damaging companies were bailed out while hospitals were underfunded. Thousands of workers were flown in to work the fields in the Global North for starvation wages, while thousands of others were denied security and the right to live.

Despite all of this, some of the measures that have been enacted in many countries around the world seemed unthinkable before the pandemic: democratic governments forced companies to produce essentials such as protective clothing and ventilators. Most aircraft were grounded. Better forms of social security were being discussed far more seriously than ever before, but they were hardly implemented anywhere. Moreover, the responses to the COVID-19 pandemic – as to many other crises in the past – have shown that **completely different developments and policies are possible and can be discussed and implemented quickly**.

Sadly, in the past two years since the original writing process, things have not improved. With the ongoing war in Yemen, the Russian invasion in the Ukraine and the brutal escalation of violence in Israel and Palestine, military conflicts are on top of the agenda. They are costing lives and worsening living conditions through destruction and the ensuing consequences such as energy and food shortages.

February 2024 was also the moment where temperatures breached the 1.5°C limit for over a year for the very first time. At the same time, right-wing parties and authoritarian regimes threaten democracies and pro-democratic movements in many parts of the world – from Milei in Argentina and Meloni in Italy to the battle against monarchy in Thailand. However, global justice movements are still present. In Germany and Austria, the bonds between trade unions and Fridays for Future are growing stronger and their joint strikes for better working conditions in the public transportation sector are now larger and more powerful. Since January 2024, millions have taken to the streets over here to defend democracy and human rights and to hinder the rise to power of the radical right.

It is impossible to know whether the future will be based on neoliberalism or authoritarianism, or whether the crises and struggles that will occur in the coming years will lead to a socio-ecological transformation – and thus toward the vision described here. Whatever the case, **we are living in a time of transformation**. Let's stand together and fight for our common future.

We hope that you enjoy reading the ideas set out here and that you will be inspired by them. More importantly, we hope that our vision will encourage you to help build a just, ecological and democratic future for all.

Anne Pinnow, Kai Kuhnhenn,

Matthias Schmelzer and Nina Treu.

– Leipzig and Berlin, May 2024 –

HOW WAS THIS VISION DEVELOPED?

We developed our vision with the help of numerous people from German-speaking countries engaged practically and theoretically in imagining emancipatory futures. Our vision builds on the results of twelve Future Workshops involving 200 pioneers from different areas of society. More information about the methodology, as well as the people and organizations involved, is available at the end of this book.

The values behind our vision

*Every vision of society is based on a particular set of values – these are the principles behind the vision and its ideas of how various aspects of society should be shaped. Below, we set out the values behind a **Future for All**. Because the terms we use can be interpreted differently, we take care to define what each one means in our context. The chapters that follow explain the ways in which these values are implemented. If you would prefer not to read the definitions, you can skip ahead to Chapter 1 and you will still understand the text.*

Needs-based society

A needs-based society puts the satisfaction of essential human needs at the center of economic activity. What, then, are "necessary needs", and how can we strike a balance between people's different needs? Needs can be defined in a variety of ways; they usually encompass physical needs such as food and warmth, but they also include community, recognition, peace and self-expression. Because different people express some of these needs more strongly than others, our vision uses democratic, creative processes to develop ways to ensure that everyone's needs can be met without disregarding those of others.

Democracy

Democracy means that everyone has the same basic human rights. A democratic society is one in which everyone can shape all the decisions that affect them. Providing people with equal social, cultural and economic rights grants everyone the same opportunities. Moreover, it also means that everyone has the same needs-based access to societal resources such as knowledge, land and the means of production.

Shapeability

Shapeability means that the society with all its structures and principles is open to change. In our vision, critique, scrutiny, creativity and change, as well as protest and resistance are encouraged and cherished.

Self-determination and freedom

A free society is one in which everyone is able to shape their own lives. People voluntarily contribute to a free society and understand that their freedom can only be guaranteed through the freedom of others. Our vision seeks to strengthen freedom and self-determination wherever doing so imposes no restriction on other people's lives. This means that society is organised around a form of freedom that encourages inclusion. Agreements and rules in society are aimed at strengthening individual self-determination and finding a balance between different people's freedoms.

Security

Security means that people no longer fear hunger, poverty, loneliness, exclusion, violence, or – if they fall ill or grow old – neglect. It means that everyone is provided with wide-ranging social security and that society assumes responsibility for protecting people's dignity and shielding them from physical harm. Finally, political and economic life in a secure society is geared towards meeting people's diverse needs.

Solidarity

Solidarity means that we can shape, manage and celebrate our lives together. Solidarity involves people recognizing that they are dependent on one another and on strengthening one another's freedom. People treat one another with respect, ensure that everyone is included in society, and collectively find ways to distribute and share society's wealth.

Foresightedness

Foresight means that we recognize our existential connections with one another as well as with non-human living beings and the natural environment. It encompasses assuming responsibility for and safeguarding the future of people and the planet. We jointly and precautiously decide on how (and how far) we intervene in nature. This includes the technologies that we use, the direction in which technologies are developed, and the consequences that they may have. Structures are shaped in a way to enable an environmentally friendly lifestyle that avoids human exploitation.

Diversity

Diversity means recognizing that everyone's different lifestyles are valid; actively encouraging diverse ways of thinking, loving, working, believing and living; and fighting against all forms of discrimination. Diversity runs through all social institutions and structures – from the neighborhood to the global level.

Why do we need a future for all?

Because contemporary society is characterized by inequalities, conflicts and existential crises, many are searching for alternatives. Critical analyses of these structural problems are the basis on which to develop transformative visions for change.

Economic and geopolitical crises

Because capitalism is unstable, it inevitably and continuously falls into crises. It produces wealth for the few at the expense of the many, undermines democracy, excludes billions of people from prosperity and dignity – all the while destroying the ecological foundations for human flourishing in the process. In its purest form, capitalism subordinates all other aims in society to the production of economic growth and the pursuit of immediate profit, regardless of people's needs. And because capitalism is based on competition, it inevitably and continuously produces conflicts, geopolitical tensions or all-out war. The wealthy and powerful appropriate resources, land and labor through colonial and neo-colonial forms of domination, often accompanied by or resulting in military confrontations.

▼

We want to live in a peaceful society with a stable, democratic and equitable economy that focuses on people's needs while also protecting nature.

A narrow understanding of democracy

Although parliamentary democracy is a great achievement, many national governments in the Global North fundamentally restrict people's opportunities to participate in and access democracy. Power, social hierarchies and discrimination prevent many from (fully) participating in democratic decision-making in any meaningful way. Such systemic exclusion leads to frustration with parliamentary politics. People with greater incomes and higher levels of formal education have more resources (such as time, money and interpersonal connections, just to name a few), which makes it easier for them to actively participate in society and democracy. At the same time, formal democratic participation is based on a narrow understanding of democracy that limits participation to a small number of issues and to electing political parties and officials.

▼

We want to live in a society in which everyone can participate equally in all decisions that affect their lives.

Hierarchy and discrimination

Today's society is characterized by power relations that divide people into categories such as male/female, white/black/person of color, queer/hetero, cis/trans, healthy/disabled, middle class/working class, Christian/Muslim/Jewish and adult/child. Whereas for some these socially constructed categories confer privilege, for most they are associated with severe, often overlapping disadvantages. This means that we are privileged or discriminated against simply because of who we are. The resulting forms of discrimination – such as racism, classism and sexism – intertwine, intersect and lead to power relations. This has an impact on all areas of life such as laws, treatment by the police and authorities, the labor market, exclusion at the individual level, sexual harassment, norms and values, and even on art and literature.

▼

We want to live in a society that is free from hierarchy and discrimination.

Rising levels of global inequality

Society is deeply divided, particularly at the global level: unfathomable wealth is concentrated in the hands of the few, while many experience unimaginable depths of poverty. Worse still, the wealth gap continues to grow. But inequality is not just about wealthy capitalists. Many people in the Global North also benefit from the "imperial way of life" – that is, a way of consuming, working and living that is based on practically unlimited global access to work and nature. The way of life in the Global North is therefore made possible at the expense of people (and nature) in other regions of the world. Nevertheless, even in the capitalist centers, where the benefits of the imperial way of life continue to accumulate, people face huge and growing inequalities. This not only flies in the face of social justice, but also widens the imbalance of power. The ludicrously unequal ownership of financial resources, living space, land and the means of production prevents billions of people from participating equally in society – this is, to say the least, deeply undemocratic. Labor is also unequally distributed; for example, care work, which is often made invisible in the political and economic sphere, is poorly paid and predominantly performed by women and People of Color.

▼

We want to live in a society that is fair and that enables everyone to participate equally.

Exploitation and the destruction of nature

Relations between people and the non-human environment are shaped by appropriation and domination. Our economy is based on the massive exploitation of nature to generate profit, achieve growth and enable people to live resource-intensive lifestyles. Increasing levels of resource usage and industrial agriculture are producing more emissions, accelerating extinction and destroying ecosystems throughout the world. Non-human life is destroyed solely for the sake of profit, and this inflicts unnecessary suffering on other living beings. Above all, companies as well as the global middle and upper classes benefit at the expense of people around the world who have very little money and even fewer privileges. Moreover, these people lack the means to protect themselves from the consequences of the climate catastrophe, soil degradation and the destruction of ecosystems.

▼

We want to live in a society that preserves the natural environment for all living beings.

Alienation, stress and anxiety

Social inequalities, power relations and the destruction of nature prevent people from living a good life, as do many of the other constraints and crises afflicting modern capitalist society. Many people undertake wage work that they consider pointless, unnecessary or even harmful. Acceleration and concentration in all areas of life is intensifying the alienation that people feel from themselves, from what they do and from others. This triggers stress, burnout and dissatisfaction. At the same time, it has also led to a permanent crisis in care work and, therefore, inadequate levels of care provision. Finally, because the economy and international relations are based on competition, people live their whole lives in fear of job loss, poverty in old age, downward social mobility, and war.

▼

We want to live in a society that enables everyone to make their own decisions and to lead a peaceful, happy and good life.

Global Justice

1

In 2048, there is:

↦ A governance of the global commons by everyone for the good of all
↦ A Council for Sustainability to democratically manage global resources

In 2048, there is no longer:

↤ (Post-)colonial inequality
↤ free trade agreements
↤ unnecessary transport

In 2048, nation states no longer play an important role in governing society. Economies are organized on a more regional level (▶ 3 Economy). Power – including power over economic decisions – lies primarily at the local and regional levels (▶ 2 Democracy). Open borders provide people with complete freedom of movement; the movement of goods and money, however, is restricted by regulations on global trade (▶ 9 Freedom of movement).

2048

Global diversity in the pluriverse

The colonial inequalities that arose over centuries have largely been levelled out – materially, financially, technologically, environmentally and ideologically. The current South–North relationship, as well as the way in which we overcame colonial structures, resulted from decades of struggle against capitalist privileges, colonial continuities and transnational corporate structures. To establish partnership-based trade, people in the Global North provided financial, cultural and political compensation for colonial crimes, ecological exploitations and climate debt – this included returning artefacts looted during colonialism. Lifestyles that were mainly found in the former Global North – which were possible only at the expense of the environment and other people, especially those living in the Global South – have disappeared in favor of simpler, more cooperative solidarity-based lifestyles. In the past, many people lived in poverty; today, everyone has a share in society's wealth. Because freedom and self-determination are essential aspects of all areas of our society, diverse and very different concepts of society with similar levels of material means exist side by side. We live in a pluriverse that accommodates many ways of living, eating, loving, producing together and collectively managing societal institutions.

Open re-localisation

This pluriverse of various modes of living in solidarity is open and in flux. It is based on the global exchange of ideas and some goods. Everyone enjoys freedom of movement (▶ 9 Freedom of movement). Environmentally harmful forms of transport have long ceased to exist, and interregional trade takes place using solar-powered ships, sailing ships and energy-efficient trains (▶ 12 Mobility and transport). What little air travel remains is reserved for people who really need it – whether for urgent family visits, important meetings or for the provision of specialist services and medical care. Because wind- and solar-powered transport is more complex and slower than the fossil-fuelled means of transport of the past, most manufacturing and consumption takes place locally (▶ 5 Manufacturing and business; ▶ 10 Food and agriculture). This also means that far fewer goods and services are traded across the globe. The basic principle is that of subsidiarity, which means that things are decided and done at the smallest possible level by those most affected by the decisions.

The economy is much more regionally focused: it is organized at a supra-regional level only when doing so benefits everyone. Since in a globally just world, companies can no longer use international trade to profit from wage and income gaps, or from tax advantages and different social and environmental regulations, many of the incentives to transport goods have vanished.

HOW CAN WE BUILD A PEACEFUL WORLD WITHOUT WEAPONS?

People have always dreamed of world peace – yet for all our dreaming, we are still far from making a peaceful world our reality. Some aspects of the issue are fairly simple: if no one had guns and if there were no weapons industry profiting from the sale and export of weapons, there would be far fewer violent conflicts and fewer casualties. Therefore, we need a worldwide campaign to stop the production of all weapons – from small arms to nuclear weapons – and to destroy those weapons that already exist. Other aspects of this issue are far more complicated: how do we move from a world characterized by nation-states and competition to one based on cooperation? What role can international organizations like the United Nations play in this transition, and how should they be integrated into global democratic institutions? We have found answers to some of these questions and have woven them into the chapters that follow. In other cases, a great deal of discussion and research still needs to take place in addition to the development of practical approaches.

In the beginning, some people in the Global North were unhappy that foods such as fresh tropical fruits were no longer available year-round, but people now appreciate the advantages associated with these changes because regional diversity in agricultural and other products has increased significantly (▶ 10 Food and agriculture).

Goods are traded over long distances only if it really makes sense and if doing so directly improves the well-being of the trading partners and regions involved. Arms trading has long since been banned. Most raw materials come from recycling and reusing materials and components. Renewable and compostable raw materials, as well as recyclable and reusable plastics, minerals and metals are separated from one another into distinct →

2024

WHAT ALREADY EXISTS IN 2024

The Seattle-to-Brussels Network:
a pan-European network founded in the aftermath of the World Trade Organization's meeting in Seattle in 1999. The network aims to scrutinize the work of the European Union and to campaign for democratic and globally fair world trade.

▸ **s2bnetwork.org**

Pluriverse:
activists and researchers use the term "pluriverse" to describe a diverse world in which there is also space for many other worlds, as well as one that links various alternatives to development. More details can be found in the book Pluriverse: A Post-Development Dictionary.

▸ **radicalecologicaldemocracy.org/pluriverse**

Anti-militarism and the peace movement:
demonstrations, direct action and conferences against the military and arms manufacturing, and for disarmament, cooperative conflict management and a peaceful world.

▸ **ipb.org**

▸ **wri-irg.org/en**

World Social Forums:
meetings of social movements held around the world for a fair society and a cooperative economy beyond capitalism.

▸ **transformadora.org**

resource cycles. Global product and recycling standards have been put in place to ensure high-quality reuse and recycling. The need for non-renewable raw materials has fallen sharply because resources are used far more efficiently now, and because far less manufacturing takes place. This has reduced to a minimum the need to extract new raw materials. Decisions as to whether new resources (such as metals required for batteries) should be mined are collectively taken in participatory processes that involve everyone who would be affected. The views of the local communities most affected by the mining are particularly important. In fact, they largely determine the conditions of extraction and trading of the raw materials, which are almost always processed in the region in which they are mined.

World trade for the good of all

Democratic institutions ensure that world trade is geared towards everyone's well-being. These institutions set trade rules and follow guiding principles that have been democratically established throughout the world. Trade among regions is environmentally friendly, solidarity-based, fair, not undertaken at the expense of others, subsidiary, promotes peace and is designed to meet people's needs.

In order to preserve the global commons – such as the atmosphere, the oceans and biological diversity – democratic institutions from neighborhoods to global levels (▸ 2 Democracy) are committed to protecting nature, respecting human rights and safeguarding social justice. Democratic institutions devise rules to ensure that trade takes place – particularly over long distances – only when it promotes these goals rather than undermining them. Companies operate cooperatively, fairly and in an environmentally sustainable way. Cooperation between manufacturing and trading partners is based on long-term contacts (▸ 5 Manufacturing and business). If prices play a role, they are negotiated between partners and reflect the social and environmental costs involved in production. However, trade largely takes place outside of markets. Instead of competition, the focus is on cooperation as well as democratic negotiation and planning processes.

Democracy

2

In 2048, there is:
↦ participation at all political levels
↦ consensus-building
↦ transparent political decision-making

In 2048, there is no longer:
↤ manipulation and dominance during debates
↤ haggling over building coalitions
↤ career politicians

Democratic principles

Our lives are characterized by self-determination at the individual, neighborhood, club, and work levels. Our society is much more equal than it was 30 years ago, and we have a communication culture that aims to find the best solution to problems together. We respect one another during debates, and we reject discrimination and prejudice. We learn early on how to facilitate meetings as well as how to lead and shape discussions. We aim for consensus and solutions that meet the needs of the majority while also protecting minorities.

2048

⭐ Our democracy is run in accordance with the following principles:

→ Every person affected by a decision can be involved in decision-making at all levels so that all may live a self-determined life. This involves using diverse procedures and processes, from sharing experiences to traditional elections and transferable votes to finding people to represent our opinion on a particular topic.

→ Decisions should be made at the lowest possible level. The principle of subsidiarity states that the greatest possible level of self-determination and personal responsibility is achieved when higher-level bodies only make decisions that cannot be taken at a lower level.

→ Democratic councils should be established in each neighborhood and region, in addition to specialist councils and political parties (see below). Anyone can take on the role of a representative, as long as their council, neighborhood or party trusts them to do so.

→ All administrative positions are rotated to ensure that many more and different types of people are involved in decision-making, even at higher levels. Council representatives can be replaced at any time at the request of the people who delegated or elected them.

→ A high level of transparency is ensured in decision-making, despite conducting elections in secret. Neighborhoods don't need to rely on reports from their representatives because discussions at all levels can be followed freely on the internet.

Neighborhoods

⭐ Neighborhoods are the most important areas in our lives. Many informal and formal discussions take place, and important decisions are made in our neighborhoods (▸ 11 Housing). The people who live in a particular neighborhood discuss their interests and make decisions in line with the rules they have decided on. Neighborhoods are also places where young people learn to discuss, compromise and incorporate other people's concerns into their own decision-making. If decisions need to be made on a larger scale, neighborhood representatives are sent to regional and higher-level councils.

DO ALL OF THESE COUNCILS MEAN THAT EVERYONE WILL BE SITTING AROUND IN MEETINGS?

If society is based on involvement in so many councils – in neighborhoods, companies, general and specific councils – will we just be sitting around in meetings all the time? There are several possible answers to this question.

1. We would need to speak more about the world we live in, instead of expecting other people (politicians, managers and bosses) to do so for us.

2. The 20-hour working week means that we would have much more time to discuss these issues than we have today (▸ 6 Employment).

3. Anyone who has ever participated in properly facilitated discussions knows that making decisions together is much easier than many people think. This is especially true when the people involved have a common goal or concern (for example, when they do not view themselves as competitors or opponents, as is often the case today). Finally, when joint decision-making processes become the norm, we will all get a lot better at them.

4. Trust develops quickly in societies built on cooperation instead of competition. Therefore, it would not be necessary for everyone to attend every single council meeting because the people who were present would take everyone's needs into account.

General councils

⭐ Even if decisions are made much closer to the places that are affected by them, higher levels are still needed when it comes to issues such as the regional distribution of living space, the intraregional rail network and the use of global commons such as water or air. Lower-level decisions are taken by neighborhood, district, village, or even regional or city councils. Councils at lower levels can send representatives to higher levels that not only make decisions, but also have the means to enforce them.

Councils are controlled from two directions. On the one hand, representatives are empowered to make decisions only to a limited extent – important decisions must be voted on by a lower-level or neighborhood council. Voting does not have to aim for a simple "yes" or "no" answer, but can also be more differentiated, such as "On a scale of 1 to 10, how strongly would you agree with this proposal?" On the other hand, councils must also respect human rights and the constitution when making their decisions (see below).

2024

Rojava:

Rojava: The Autonomous Administration of North and East Syria is built on decentralized social structures and democratic confederalism according to Abdullah Öcalan

‣ **wikipedia.org: Rojava**

‣ **wikipedia.org: Democratic confederalism**

Workers' councils:

Councils have a long tradition and they have been established during many social upheavals, such as during the Paris Commune in 1871, the initial phase of the Soviet Union (in Russian "Soviet" means council), the German November Revolution of 1918/1919 and in Poland and East Germany in 1989.

‣ **wikipedia.org : Soviet republic**

Parecon – participatory economics:

This is a model of a participatory economy in which councils and self-government play a central role.

‣ **participatoryeconomics.info**

Liquid Democracy:

This is a mixed form of indirect and direct democracy used by many organizations and political parties to make some of their decisions.

‣ **wikipedia.org : Liquid democracy**

Radical Ecological Democracy:

framework emerging out of learnings from grassroots and policy initiatives in India such as Kalvapriksh and Vikalp Sangam (meaning "Alternatives confluence" in Hindi).

‣ **radicalecologicaldemocracy.org**

‣ **kalpavriksh.org**

‣ **vikalpsangam.org**

Specialist councils

★ In addition to general councils, we also have specialist councils at all levels focused on specific issues. We have councils that are responsible for areas such as the supply of electricity, equality, and the organization of work. If necessary, they discuss issues with other councils (perhaps the Housing Council needs to contact the Mobility Council). Specialist councils seek to involve not only experts, but also other stakeholders such as staff, consumers and local residents.

Councils in companies

★ All companies are run by their staff. This means that all decisions within companies are made jointly by the people who work there, or by their chosen delegates. In some companies, the interests of other stakeholders, such as consumers and suppliers, are also represented. The general and specialized councils monitor companies' manufacturing (e.g. is production sustainable and fair?) as well as the products they produce (e.g. does society actually need the things that we are producing, and, if so, do our products fit their purpose?).

THE DEMOCRACY OF THE FUTURE – SOLVING A PUZZLE

We found it difficult to describe what democracy might look like in the year 2048. It was clear to us that people should be more involved in decision-making and that they should also have the time they need to do so. We also think that a different form of political debate is needed. Beyond this, many questions remain unanswered: Should we preserve our current political system in the hope that a different economic system will lead the old institutions to adapt and develop a different type of politics? Should we favor a council system, given that councils appear to spring up naturally wherever they are needed? Should we call "councils" by another name because many people associate councils with negative connotations? How can participation, openness to change and basic public services all be guaranteed? Who enforces such guarantees and which means (of power) should they have to do so? Can these structures be designed on the drawing board, or do they need to emerge organically as part of a process? These as yet unanswerable questions mean that our reports from 2048 should be regarded as first steps aimed at encouraging debate.

Parliament and constitutional convention

⭐ We have various supra-regional and trans-regional parliaments, as well as political parties that can be elected and send representatives to parliament. Parliaments are tasked mainly with higher-level decision-making; however, weighty decisions must be supported by the results of referenda. Parliaments also ensure compliance with the constitution. In addition to the protection of minorities, this includes ensuring the provision of basic public services, as enshrined in the European Constitution that was passed at the end of the 2020s. To do so, parliaments also have the opportunity to intervene in various councils. This usually consists of communicative conflict resolution mechanisms based on restorative justice with the aim of repairing material and immaterial damage and restoring positive social relationships.

Constitutions are regularly amended by constitutional conventions.

WILL IT ALL BE "PEACE, LOVE AND HARMONY" OR WILL THERE BE CONFLICTS IN UTOPIA?

Wherever people live together, there are conflicts. This will also be the case in 2048. But the reasons why they occur and the way in which they are dealt with would be very different in 2048. In 2048, everyone enjoys a good life and is part of a society that no longer exploits the natural environment (▸ The values behind our vision). As such, many of the reasons behind much of the suffering and the conflicts that occurred in 2024 are no longer relevant. This means that there are fewer conflicts, and those that do occur tend not to threaten people's livelihoods.

We are shaped by the society in which we live. People are not naturally selfless or egoistic; nor are they necessarily peaceful or aggressive. Rather, the shared environment in which we live promotes certain characteristics. People who experience love, recognition, honesty, care and attentiveness from an early age grow up differently from those who experience ignorance, hate, oppression and, violence. Therefore, a society promoting characteristics and attitudes that are conducive to solidarity will have a positive impact on people's personalities, and vice versa. Our vision sets out a society, which relies on these same positive feedback loops.

In order to deal appropriately with the conflicts that do arise, we would need to establish and implement forms of communication that enable people to fully participate in discussions about their needs. The aim is to ensure that everyone is in a position to understand what the discussions are about. Over time, everyone learns to recognize the actual needs behind people's views and strategies, and how these can be communicated. At the same time, societies also need spaces where people can share their experiences, where their needs are listened to, and where their needs can be weighed up equally against those of others. This applies on a personal basis in close relationships as much as to the political and economic levels during debates in the councils described above.

Our vision relies on a social approach to conflicts. We advocate conflict transformation through reparation instead of exclusion and punishment. There are no prisons in our vision. Instead, we have spaces and social groups that support people in making amends for the injuries and damage they have caused. The aim is to use restorative justice to reestablish positive, functioning social relationships. Participation, empowerment and accountability ensures that society takes responsibility for the conditions it creates. Our society relies on facilitators (trained in communication, trust-building and de-escalation) instead of heavily armed police. Discussion and negotiation remain the best and most important strategies, even in violent conflicts.

Economy

3

In 2048, there is:
↦ a large share of the economy self-organized as a gift economy
↦ regulation in place to make sure all remaining markets are
   committed to the common good
↦ an expanded care sector
↦ regional economic structures

In 2048, there is no longer:
← economic activity that is purely profit-oriented
← an arms industry, advertising or insurance companies
← planned obsolescence
← private ownership of larger means of production

From market dominance to democratic self-determination

In 2048, economies consist of three pillars: (1) the self-organized commons, (2) public and democratic basic services, and (3) markets focused on the common good. What does this mean, and how did it come about?

The crises culminating in the beginning of the 21st century – climate, biodiversity, inequality, austerity, conflicts – showed that markets and the structures encompassing the growth-based economy were failing to meet many people's basic needs. While this system was making some people richer and more powerful, it did not provide affordable housing, environmental protection or proper health care to all. Furthermore, it resulted in increasing insecurity and division, as well as a lack of participation in society and leisure time. In response to public pressure, many districts and cities decided to seize control of housing, mobility and energy, or to hand such control over to democratically run companies such as collectives and cooperatives. More and more self-run alternatives emerged, such as solidarity-based and community supported agricultural projects, which form part of the gift economy and work largely free of charge. Gift economies have no form of direct exchange; everyone produces for the community and is in turn supplied by it. Instead of exchanging products on the market, they are made available to everyone on a needs-basis.

This trend of pushing back against markets in favour of self-organized alternatives and the public provision of basic services has increased continuously, yet is not complete in 2048. →

Today, our economy is aimed at improving people's well-being instead of increasing profit, promoting growth and maximizing production indiscriminately. Economic activity is geared toward meeting specific needs such as sustenance, housing, communication and participation in an ecological, social and democratic manner. The goal is both to provide goods and services and to enable us to participate and shape society, to be active and pursue a profession.

2048

2024

WHAT ALREADY EXISTS IN 2024

Economy for the common good:
Economic activity contributes to the common good, and success is measured by the common-good product (economy), the common good balance sheet (business), and the common-good audit (investments).
▸ **web.ecogood.org**

Solidarity economy:
Business is conducted to meet people's needs using cooperation and self-organization. This is done in a way that is as environmentally friendly, non-discriminatory and globally just as possible. It involves prioritising utility over profit, and cooperation over competition
▸ **ripess.org**

Commons:
The commons encompass common use, production, management and development beyond state and markets. Processes of commoning can focus on anything from food production, programming and the shared use of sustainable energy sources to solving transport problems and caring.
▸ **iasc-commons.org**

Degrowth or post-growth:
Degrowth describes a transformational path toward a good life for all, emphasizing that a social-ecological transformation in wealthy countries in the Global North goes hand-in-hand with democratically organized reductions in manufacturing and consumption to a globally just and sustainable level.
▸ **degrowth.info**

Gift economies:
These economies are based on the principles of contribution instead of private ownership, equal exchange or bartering.
▸ **routledge.com**

Exploring Economics:
This is a network and open-access e-learning platform about pluralist economics. It supports the study of a variety of economic theories, methods and topics, from feminist to Keynesian to Marxist economics.
▸ **exploring-economics.org**

NOW-NET Network on Economic Transformation [Netzwerk Oekonomischer Wandel]:
German-speaking representatives of Commons, Solidarity Economy, Degrowth, Economy for the Common Good, Gift Economy as well as Collaborative and Co-creative Economy have joined together to represent in diversity what unites them: a future-friendly alternative to the ruling economic order.
▸ **now-net.org**

→ Specifically, everyone today has guaranteed access to *comprehensive basic public services*, which enables full participation in society (▸ 4 Social security).

Markets play a far more minor role in society now and they have been aligned to people's needs and the common good through regulation and democratization. The number of people now active in the self-organized commons continues to grow (▸ 5 Manufacturing and business).

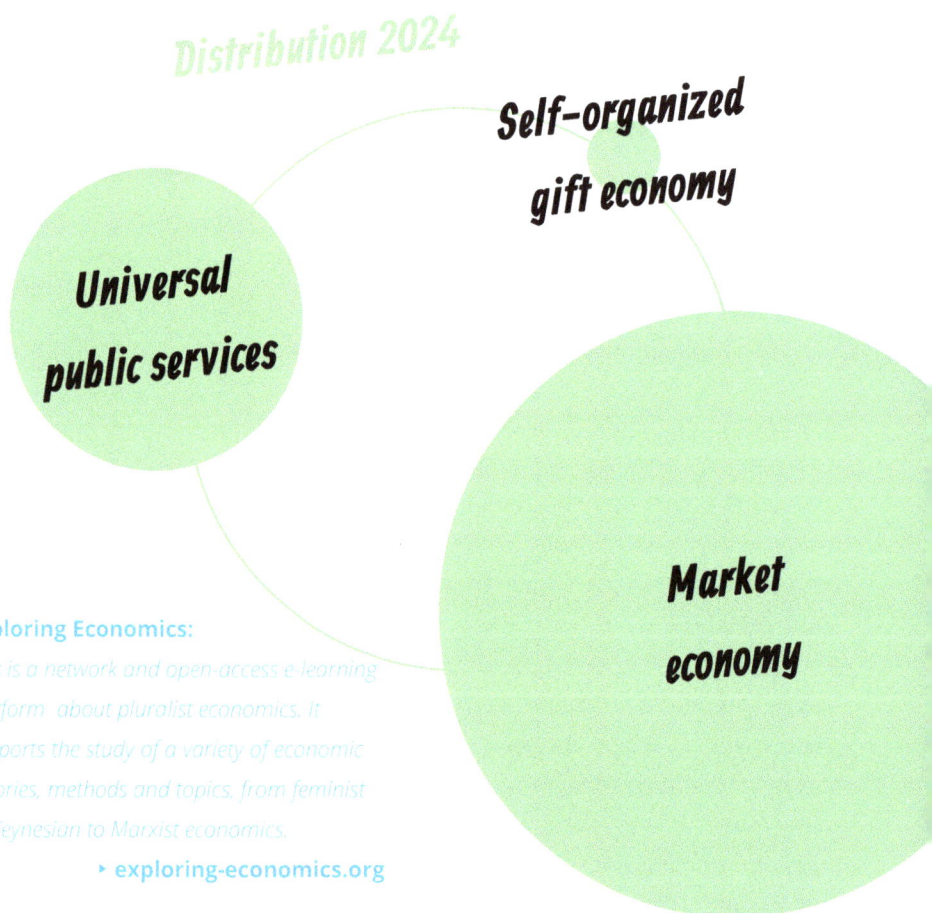

Distribution 2024

Universal public services

Self-organized gift economy

Market economy

This figure depicts the economy in 2024 (above) and how it is now in 2048 (right).

The sectoral structure of the economy

Because the economy is now focused on meeting people's material as well as immaterial needs, it has a fundamentally different structure than it had during the 2020s.

Care work such as nursing, health care and education is now at the heart of all economic activity (▸ 6 Employment). This has led to a massive expansion of the care sector (▸ 8 Health and participation). Whereas in the past, people working in these sectors faced poor working conditions and low wages, everyone now understands that care work forms the foundation of society. Consequently, many more people are now active in these areas, the work is held in high esteem by society at large, and – when organized as waged work – care activities pay a good salary (▸ 5 Manufacturing and business).

Other areas have remained important, such as agriculture, power generation and engineering. In contrast to the past, production and manufacturing are now sustainable and fair, and we only make products that are useful to society. This is very different from the resource-intensive industrial manufacturing of decades past, which has been scaled back sharply. As such, the share of heavy, automotive, mining or construction industry is very small indeed. Entire branches of industry – as well as some services that were not meeting people's essential needs – have become redundant or have simply disappeared. These include the arms industry, advertising and insurance companies, as well as large parts of the financial sector (▸ 15 Finance).

In some cases, democratic decisions have led to restrictions on the variety of products that are available. Planned obsolescence and rapidly changing fashions are a thing of the past. However, decentralized economic structures, regional differences in the use of resources and particular needs as well as culture and tradition have led to a much greater variety of products, materials or processes in some other areas, such as construction.

Overall, economic structures now tend to be much more regional than they were in the past. Most things are now produced at the regional level, and goods are only transported over long distances if absolutely necessary (▸ 1 Global justice). Cross-regional trade is carried out by cooperative organizations, such as companies controlled and managed by their staff; consumer and producer cooperatives, companies in public ownership, global networks of bodies administrating the commons, technical-scientific cooperatives, and many more (▸ 4 Social security).

Distribution 2048

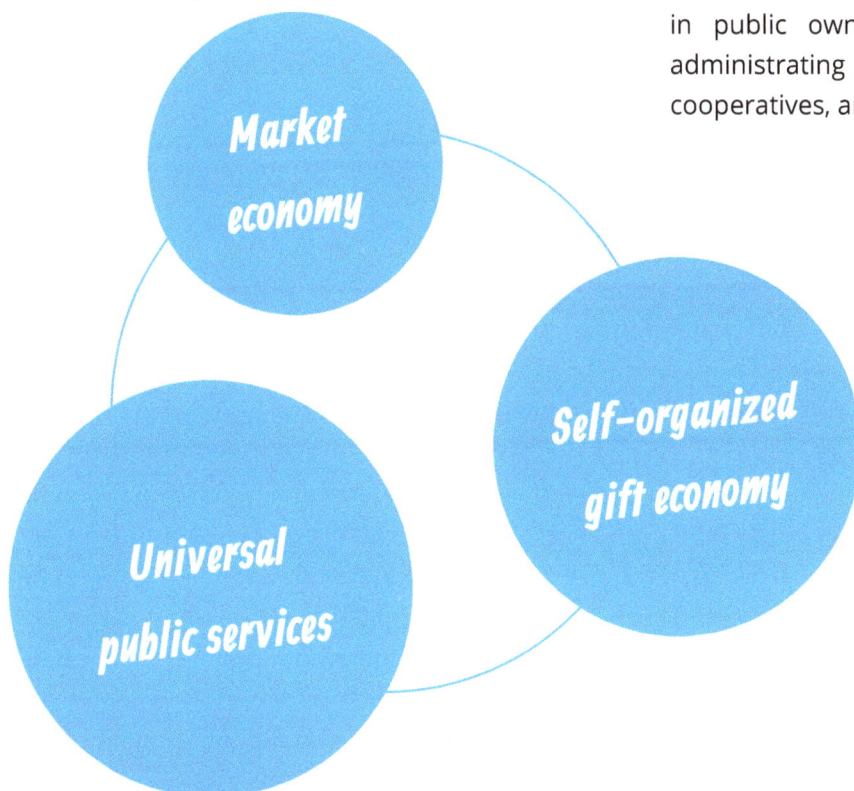

Market economy

Self-organized gift economy

Universal public services

WHY DO MARKETS STILL EXIST IN UTOPIA?

Markets have been heavily criticized as organizational and distributional mechanisms – and rightly so. They result in the unequal distribution of wealth and make access to basic necessities such as food and shelter dependent on personal income and wealth. In some ways, markets are the antithesis of the needs-based economy that we are advocating. They are nevertheless part of our vision, albeit in a fundamentally different form than today's markets. In 2048, markets have only limited power, and they are democratically regulated to ensure that they work for the common good. They also constitute only one relatively small aspect of a much larger economy: in addition to markets, we have publicly provided basic services and a self-organized gift economy.

This hypothetical situation raises several questions:

→ *Can markets really be adapted so comprehensively as to ensure that they focus on the common good? And if so, wouldn't we need a powerful state to enforce wide ranging controls and regulations and to ensure that this remains the case (which would raise a few other questions)?*

→ *Is it truly possible to fully internalize all market costs – and, if so, would it be ethical to do so? Are "prices that reflect the true social and environmental costs" only a theoretical dream of economics? And if so, are measures to come close to this dream still useful?*

→ *Is it possible to have markets in some sectors of the economy when public utilities and self-organized commons are proliferating in other areas? Or will the market eventually penetrate all areas of life and all economic sectors?*

Social Security

4

Today, we enjoy extensive social security provisions that enables all of us to live without fear and ensure that everyone can participate in society throughout their entire life. Everyone is entitled to these services, regardless of any conditions or other income that they may have. Benefit levels are set democratically (▸ 2 Democracy) and vary by region. They are universally valid within a particular region, such as individual rights, and sufficient to meet people's basic needs. Many regions have divided social security provisions into two components: (1) full access to public infrastructure and services, and (2) additionally a financial freedom guarantee.

2048

Infrastructure and services

✦ Today, everyone has access to the infrastructure and services they need to lead good lives. These include:

→ Health and care (▸ 8 Health and participation)

→ Child care, education and further training (▸ 6 Employment, 14 Education)

→ Public infrastructure such as streets, parks, public buildings, Centers of Life or Community Centers, cultural institutions, sports facilities and libraries (▸ 11 Housing)

→ Local and regional public transport, which has been significantly expanded (▸12 Mobility & Transport)

→ Housing (democratically allocated space, with exceptions for people with special needs ▸11 Housing)

→ Water, energy and heat (a democratically determined amount for each person, with exceptions for special needs (▸13 Energy & Climate)

→ Internet and communication, including one comprehensive digital device (▸7 Technology)

Financial freedom

Everyone receives an unconditional, tax-free and monetary basic income. The aim is to enable people to meet any of their needs that are not covered by the free infrastructure and basic services. These might include:

→ Types of food that go beyond people's basic needs and a self-organized gift economy
→ Clothing
→ Sustainable forms of transport, such as bicycles
→ Leisure activities and cultural events that are not available free of charge
→ Major trips and holidays
→ Visits to restaurants and cafés

People who have greater requirements than the (democratically defined) standards on living space, heating, energy and water can also use their basic income to cover the progressively increasing fees of these goods and services.

The infrastructure, services and basic income provided to everyone ensure that we all have comprehensive social security coverage. At the same time, the working week has been reduced to a maximum of 20 hours (▸ 6 Employment) because meeting people's needs is often less about gaining material goods than a question of having enough time for care work, leisure, political participation, learning and socializing.

2024

WHAT ALREADY EXISTS IN 2024

BIEN – Basic Income Earth Network:
Global Network for the introduction of an unconditional basic income.

▸ **basicincome.org**

UBIE – Unconditional Basic Income Europe:
European network of activists and initiatives campaigning for the introduction of an unconditional basic income in Europe and the recognition of basic income as a universal human right.

▸ **eci-ubi.eu**

UBI Taiwan:
Universal Basic Income in Taiwan, which is now granted yearly to each citizen.

▸ **ubitaiwan.org**

WAIT, IF SO MUCH IS AVAILABLE FOR FREE, WHO WOULD BOTHER TO WORK?

In our vision, nobody has to work to get what they need – everyone is provided with enough material and immaterial goods to lead a good life, no matter how much they work. However, in every society, certain types of work have to be done, and done urgently, if everyone is to be able to live a good life: People must be cared for and they require food and heating. If we were to live in a society in which no one needed to work, how could we ensure that such vital work would still get done?

The answer to this question depends on our view of humanity: Are people egoists who care only about themselves, or are they empathic beings with a natural need to care for others? We believe that people can be both: It just depends on the society in which they live – and societies are shaped by people. All essential forms of work will be done voluntarily in a society that permits people to freely choose what they want to do and how they should do it, particularly if people receive proper recognition for the work they do – including (or, indeed, especially) jobs that are often considered unpleasant. In fact, there will probably be very few jobs that everyone finds unpleasant. And if some important work were to remain undone, technical and social solutions can be put in place to encourage people to do so – work can be rotated or the people who undertake these tasks can be paid particularly well.

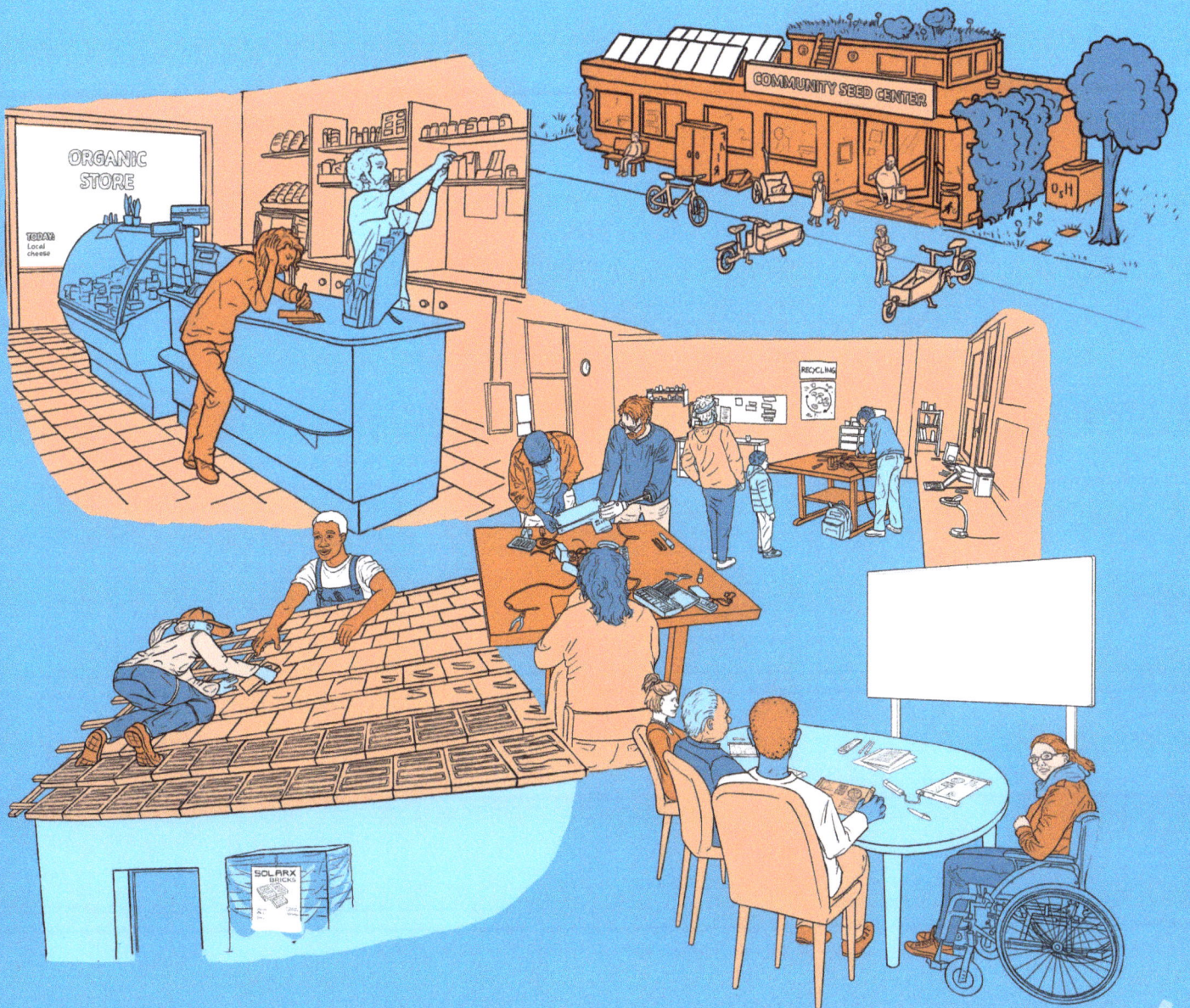

Manufacturing & Companies

5

In 2048, there is:

↦ a democratic structure to companies
↦ commoning
↦ time to show appreciation for other's work

In 2048, there is no longer:

↞ the need to work to secure a livelihood
↞ highly unequal wages
↞ profits from land ownership
↞ capital and profit-oriented stock corporations

Democratic and fair workplaces

Today, goods and services are produced by a variety of company forms. Companies are organizations that serve society by meeting people's needs while preserving the natural environment.

2048

Today, all companies are run and organized democratically. At the very least, this means that staff decide together what they want to manufacture and how. However, these decisions are also embedded within society: councils determine the framework within which companies can make decisions (▸ 2 Democracy). And to ensure that decision-making works well, larger companies are divided into organizational units with no more than 300 staff.

As we no longer need to undertake paid work to secure a livelihood, our companies are meaningful places for self-development and learning (▸ 14 Education) that provide only goods and services that people actually need. The work week has been reduced to a maximum of 20 hours and work has also been slowed down, leaving enough time to be involved in decisions concerning our workplaces and mutual appreciation of other's work.

In cases where remuneration is provided in the form of wages, everyone receives a similar amount. Due to an income limit, the wage cap is much lower than in the past. The income limit was set by a democratic decision taken at the regional level. In fact, the income limit has been continuously reduced over the years, and in many areas it is the same as the basic income we all receive. This means that in these places, no one can have more than twice the income of anyone else. There are no other means of generating an income (e.g. through the ownership of land, real estate, capital). Companies are taxed using environmental criteria.

Companies can network at the regional and global level. This ensures that even intricate goods such as pacemakers, digital devices and solar ships can be manufactured using complex production networks.

Diversity: Social and public companies, cooperatives and commons

Despite their similarities, there are also differences between the types of companies that have emerged over time. At one end of the spectrum, we still have some businesses that are like those that existed in the past. However, they are now democratically organized and operate with a different goal: instead of aiming to make a profit, they aim to meet people's needs. Staff are still paid wages and the products and services they offer are sold on the market. At the other end of the spectrum, we have companies run by consumers, staff, neighbors and other interest groups. These operate through self-organized processes of production, organization, caring and using. We refer to this as "commoning." These companies decide whether they pay salaries and whether they want to sell their products (within the barter economy) or work with other companies as part of the gift economy. People involved in the gift economy do so voluntarily because they understand the value of doing so. For this to work well, we had to $\longrightarrow$

2024

WHAT ALREADY EXISTS IN 2024

Collective companies:
People decide together what is produced, and how.

▸ wikipedia.org : Syndicalism

Suma Wholefoods:
A food cooperative in UK. The company is owned and run by its employees. Everyone earns the same wages, and has an equal say.

▸ suma.coop

Public welfare companies:
These companies create and focus their work on common good balance sheets, not on profit.

▸ ecogood.org

Community supported everything (CSX):
Extends the principle of solidarity-based manufacturing and consumer communities in agriculture (community supported agriculture) to other areas.

▸ communitygarden.org

Public enterprises:
These entities can be anything from libraries to waterworks that provide society with services and goods.

→ learn to treat each other as equals – especially during disputes. New methods were also created to define the extent to which particular products and services were actually needed. Very different solutions evolved through the years, from complex digital tools to traditional blackboards.

Finally, some businesses are publicly owned by villages, cities and regions and are primarily responsible for providing *social infrastructure* such as mobility, health, education, energy and culture.

Employment

6

In 2048, there is:

↦ recognition of the importance of care work

↦ enjoyment in being active

↦ time prosperity

↦ a 20-hour work week

↦ an equal division of labor

In 2048, there is no longer:

↤ pressure to work

↤ unemployment

↤ burnouts or meaningless jobs

Today, our lives are much more varied than they were in the past, and they are also much slower. The 20-hour working week means that everyone has time for themselves as well as a lot more leisure time. We are less stressed and not even under any pressure to work. This means that we are much freer to decide what we want to do with our lives.

2048

Wage labour is just one form of work among others

Today, wage labor is viewed as equally valuable as any of the three other dimensions of life: care work/ reproductive work, self-development and political involvement.

Most of us still usually work 20 hours a week. And this is enough time to guarantee that society is well-organized and has everything that it needs. In the past, "wage labor" was often equated with "employment." People even made wage labor the cornerstone of their lives. Although it contributed to survival, it did not necessarily provide people with a livelihood. Furthermore, other forms of work remained hidden. Our society is no longer so short-sighted and acknowledges how important it is that people are involved in different types of work.

"Care work" refers to activities such as cleaning, laundry, cooking, shopping and running a household. It also refers to looking after and caring for children, the elderly and other people who need support. It encompasses self-care and providing advice to friends. Self-development refers to learning, curiously exploring life, creativity, sports, writing, travelling and all other forms of leisure. Political involvement means people are participating in shaping society, such as through councils or cooperative enterprises.

Care work – centering reproductive principles and activities

Although each of the four dimensions of life is viewed as equally important (largely because we have transformed our economy to focus on meeting people's needs), care and welfare work meets a larger proportion of people's existential needs. Therefore, these areas are prioritized. This focus has resulted in profound changes to our economy. Many jobs that were performed predominantly by men are no longer necessary (the automotive industry, mining, oil-based industries, armaments manufacturing, etc.). This has led people to focus on other dimensions of life (▸ 3 Economy). This transformation was challenging, and it required a great deal of sensitivity because it led to changes in wage labor, which was one of the most important aspects of a person's identity at the time. Today, far more people of all genders undertake paid and unpaid care work. In turn, this has changed gender roles and accelerated emancipation from traditional divisions of labor. The centrality of care work has also had a significant impact on global care chains: we do not need them anymore, because we no longer have a shortage of carers. Today, it is unimaginable that anyone would be forced to leave their family and loved ones for years (in the past, it was women from the Global South who did so) to work for low wages looking after children or the elderly in other people's families far from home.

2024

WHAT ALREADY EXISTS IN 2024

Network Care Revolution:
The network promotes a new model of care relationships and a care economy in Germany.

▸ **care-revolution.org**

Hot or Cool:
This public interest think tank that explores how putting care at the heart of our societies could promote social justice while preventing ecological breakdown.

▸ **hotorcool.org**

Respect:
A Europe-wide network founded in 1998 with the aim of organising migrant women in paid domestic work and defending their rights – regardless of their residence status.

▸ **respectberlin.org**

The weight of housework is carried by many shoulders

Today, we ensure that housework is distributed among more people than it was in the past. The 20-hour week, the focus on care work and the dissolving gender roles has resulted in an equal distribution of housework between humans. At the same time, the changes made to our living spaces has led people in the same building or neighborhood to share shopping, cooking, washing, cleaning, repairing, caring of children, elderly and people with disabilities. Because housing can often be adapted to people's circumstances, most houses and blocks of flats now have large, shared kitchens, workshops, laundry rooms, common areas and gardens.

We see our neighbors much more often than people did in the past and we also have far stronger community relations. We look after our neighbors, and we support and care for them. We also bring each other food and products from the Centers of Life in neighborhoods (▸ 11 Housing), cook for each other in shared accommodation and keep our places clean and in good condition. We decide who we want to live with, who we would like to care for, and how we want to participate in the community. Today, we are embedded in our immediate neighborhoods far more than people were in the past, and we feel much less isolated as a result.

WHO SAID IT?

The sociologist Frigga Haug developed the 4-in-1 perspective – a feminist model of organizing work – that strongly inspired this chapter. Haug defines four dimensions of life that encompass individual well-being and societal involvement: employment, reproduction, personal development, and politics. Haug argued that each of the four dimensions should be equally present (4-in-1) in everyone's daily lives.

Life beyond wage labour

Most people are not involved in all four dimensions of life at the same time during the day. Rather, we tend to pursue one or two dimensions more actively during particular phases of our lives. This leads the focus of our lives to change continuously. We might concentrate on education for a while before pursuing our interests in a particular area. This could be followed by caring responsibilities and a phase of political involvement. We might then take on wage work before going back into politics. We can change from one area to another whenever we want to because no one expects us to have followed a particular "career" path. This is all possible because of the comprehensive social security that we all have – even when we do not undertake paid work (▶ 4 Social security).

Decoupling wage labor from a secure livelihood turned out to be a breakthrough in the socio-ecological transformation of society. It buried the obligation to work, and enabled people to participate in society, no matter what they do. Some people do not work at all, but this usually only happens for a short period (▶ 5 Manufacturing and business, see box). The transformation to a society without an obligation to work – but that provides people with numerous opportunities to undertake useful activities, attractive working conditions and creative opportunities – has led most people to actually want to work. However, not everyone works in the commercial sector; they take on other tasks instead. Moreover, people are more willing to contribute to society today because doing so makes sense and they can decide when and how they want to do so.

Conversation between Robert and Mandy

while clearing out the basement of the Sisyphus Working Group building.

MANDY: *I think we can get rid of all of this paperwork.*

Yesterday's work

ROBERT: *I'm not sure, Mandy. I think there are real gems here: memos, emails, reports. Look at this one: "Therefore, we conclude that Mr. Peters is unlikely to achieve his long-term performance goals in his role as key accounts manager".*

M: *Oh no, poor Mr. Peters! The language they used back then is terrible! All those hierarchies! Even when I was in the middle of it, I found it unbearable.*

R: *Here's another one: "Talent relationship management involves the management of our relationship with potential employees". I think there's a lot to unpack in that one; especially the idea that relationships have to be managed!*

M: *This one's horrible too: "Since we can assume that the labour market is a buyers' market, there is no need to prioritize imminent layoffs".*

R: *What does that even mean?*

M: *That there were so many unemployed people, they didn't have to take care of their staff.*

R: *But how can anyone be unemployed? There's always so much to do!*

M: *That's the grace of late birth! Back then, the only work that counted was paid work. And we were usually paid so little that we had to work a lot.*

R: *So, I guess the "unemployed" did the care work and were involved in politics?*

M: *No, not at all. They were expected to do everything possible to get a job. And in the meantime, they were repeatedly told that they were worthless.*

R: *So who did the care and political work back then?*

M: *Care work was done mostly by groups that were discriminated against, like women or people from other countries. Political work was outsourced to elites. So you can imagine what happened!*

R: *There is something almost elegant about the terrible way in which it all fitted together. Maybe we should analyze all of these papers and use them to write a tragicomedy!*

Technology

7

In 2048, there is:

↦ technology geared towards our needs
↦ decentralized and self-run infrastructure
↦ equal access to technology for all
↦ participatory and practically relevant research
↦ a relationship between humans and machines
  that people shape democratically

In 2048, there is no longer:

↤ environmental destruction by and for technology
↤ profit-oriented technology (development)

Understandable, people-friendly technology

Today, we have access to technology that makes our lives easier. This technology is adapted to our needs and living conditions; we understand how it works, and it is fully repairable. To ensure that technology is environmentally sustainable, the devices that we use are different from those of the past. We have far fewer devices that require high levels of resources and energy to produce and use. Furthermore, the technology that we do have is distributed fairly and equally.

★ Everyone can use technology without needing to worry about being spied upon or manipulated. Most devices are designed to be developed and used without extensive training or access to specialized resources. They can be produced and repaired in local workshops by everyone who has familiarized themselves with them. This applies to consumer goods and the means of production. Generally, low-tech solutions such as bicycles and solar thermal energy are the main technologies in use because they tend to be more efficient as well as easier to understand and repair. More complicated forms of technology are only used if society considers them necessary, such as high-tech in some areas of medicine.

2048

A digital device for all

⭐ Everyone has access to a modular, multifunctional, versatile and adaptable digital end device. People understand how these devices work and can configure them themselves. We use them to communicate with one another, write texts, decrypt data, calculate figures, take photos, listen to music and much more. They are available in different formats and sizes, and can be connected to extensions such as screens, devices for work and for playing music. We share the rest of our devices with other people, which is why we do not miss private ownership of numerous devices (▸ 11 Housing).

Privacy instead of massive data collection for profit

⭐ Data is no longer collected without consent, and we no longer have companies dedicated to amassing data about private individuals for profit. Rather, data is collected sparingly, only when needed, and with the consent of the individuals concerned. At the same time, all data, except for personal details, is made accessible to everyone. Once consent has been gained, this data can also be used for decentralized democratic planning. However, the protection of people's personal details takes precedence over efficiency.

2024

WHAT ALREADY EXISTS IN 2024

Chaos Computer Club:
the largest European hacker association, which has been a mediator in the field of technical and social developments for more than thirty years.

▸ **ccc.de/en**

Free Software Foundation:
supports people in the self-determined use of technology

▸ **fsfe.org/index.en.html**

Open Knowledge Foundation:
uses technologies, tools and events to promote open knowledge and democratic participation.

▸ **okfn.org**

Open Source Ecology:
builds open-source hardware within an open-source economy to optimize production and distribution while regenerating the environment and promoting social justice

▸ **opensourceecology.org**

Low Tech Magazine:
underscores the potential of past and often forgotten technologies and how they can inform sustainable energy practices.

▸ **lowtechmagazine.com**

London Mining Network:
supports communities harmed by London-based mining companies

▸ **londonminingnetwork.org**

Technological development to meet people's needs

⭐ Today, the relationship between humans and machines is determined democratically by people. We no longer have unnecessary technological development or digitization undertaken solely for profit. Effective mechanization and the use of digital services has made heavy physical work easier, and provides us with support when undertaking essential activities; this has also increased the quality of our products. As such, we no longer need to adapt our lives to the requirements of machines; rather, machines are adapted to meet our needs. For example, we can use machines to stir the dough for making bread, but only if the bakery staff want it and they set the rhythm, not the machine. Technology is developed together with the people who use it through participatory, practically relevant research. Manufacturing processes are made transparent for everyone. Software and hardware are open-source and can therefore be further developed by users based on open standards. This is made possible by decentralized, self-organized infrastructure. Proprietary software no longer exists, and all patents have been abolished.

Recycling and the circular economy

⭐ Almost all of the raw materials needed to manufacture technology are recycled. Very few raw materials are mined, and when mining does take place, it is done sustainably, under good working conditions, and with the consent of the local population. The resulting raw materials are distributed equitably around the world (▸ 1 Global justice). All existing devices form part of the circular economy; there is no electrical waste. Today, electronic devices last much longer than they used to, and they can be sorted for recycling once they reach the end of their life.

Engineering
News Feed 14.2.2042

Improved wash cycle

The Queer-Tech IT collective has rolled out a software upgrade for all standard washing machines as of version 3.4. The update can be downloaded from any local community server. Upgraded washing machines use 8% less energy for normal washes and the washing is still as clean as ever.

Freetext format selected

The European IT Council has stipulated that all recognized office software should support the Open Spreadsheet standard (RFC 13548). This standard simplifies the development of open software ecosystems and enables users to contribute to the further development of workplace software.

Welsh translations available

The Babylon Interpretation Group has published Welsh translations of the instructions supplied with all standard equipment. They can be found on any local community server.

Faster processors can be produced sustainably

The municipal workshop in Brno (Czech Republic) has demonstrated an environmentally friendly process that could be used to produce faster processors, which use fewer resources. This opens the door to an additional processor update. Under pressure from environmental and social organizations, the global IT Council banned the production of the latest generation of processors because of their adverse environmental impact. Because the new processor uses the rare-earth element Yttrium, the IT Council has started talks with the Recycling Council to work out how much Yttrium can be mined sustainably.

WHY ARE WE MORE SKEPTICAL ABOUT TECHNOLOGY THAN THE MAINSTREAM?

Questions such as when technology is necessary, how it should be used and who should be able to make these decisions are controversial issues – particularly when they involve digitization. There are two reasons why we do not believe that digitization automatically leads to improvements of our lives. First, technology is never neutral; it is an expression of power relations. If we want to make technology democratic, we must simplify it so that more people can make, understand and control it. Second, even if digitization were to increase efficiency, this does not automatically lead to a more sustainable economy. When efficiency increases take place without social change, they often lead to an increased number and size of devices (a rebound effect) that undermines the gains. Furthermore, digital systems consume an enormous amount of resources. If technology is to become sustainable instead of dominating our lives, we do not necessarily need more digitization – rather, we need a completely different form of technology – and we must use democracy to ensure that technology serves people's needs and therefore truly improves our lives.

Health & Participation

8

In 2048, there is:

↦ equal medical care for all

↦ self-governing medical centers

↦ accessibility

↦ full and equal participation in society for people with disabilities

↦ an equitable distribution of housework

In 2048, there is no longer:

↤ low-pay in the care sector

↤ hospitals that must be "provitable"

↤ poverty for people with physical, mental or cognitive impairments

↤ women's double burden

Today we all have equal access to holistic medical care. People with disabilities can decide how they want to live their lives and they receive everything that they need to do so. People who work in the care sector have time for their patients and have good working conditions that they set themselves.

2048

The healthcare sector

▶ Our health centers (formerly called hospitals) are bright public buildings with calm atmospheres. They are filled with people who speak different languages. They no longer merely provide health care, but also offer health education such as informational events about the body and health, sport as well as social and legal advice. Because medical care is part of the social security provided to everyone free of charge (▶ 4 Social security), everyone – regardless of their financial situation or background – receives the same standard of care.

Every district and large village has its own (albeit smaller) health center. The staff understand the local area and its particularities. They know what people in the area are dealing with and what is good for their health, but also what makes them ill. Patients are viewed holistically and preventive medicine is used to help prevent illness. This has drastically reduced the costs of healthcare. When people are sick, decisions are taken together with patients about the form of medical treatment that they should receive. If a patient prefers, the people close to them can be involved in their care and provided with accommodation to ensure that they can spend their entire time with the patient.

Like almost all institutions today, health centers are self-governing. The staff set their own working hours and shape their working conditions. All professionals in health centers work closely together – this includes social workers, translators and interpreters, cleaning and nursing staff, psychologists, physiotherapists and doctors. They all acknowledge the value of each other's work and understand that they all contribute to the health of society and people's well-being. This has led most health centers to pay all their staff the same wages.

People are much healthier today than they used to be. "Diseases of civilization" have declined significantly because life is more balanced and we are exposed to far fewer environmental toxins. We are also much less worried about downward social mobility, face less frustration and stress, and experience fewer burnouts.

A self-determined life for all

Today, society no longer limits people that have physical, psychological or cognitive impairments. Everyone is able to shape their own lives and everyone has what they need to participate in the way that best reflects their needs. This can include support from an assistant of their choice, if necessary (the assistant can also choose whom they would like to assist).

Assistance is understood holistically and encompasses all areas of life, including what used to be referred →

2024

WHAT ALREADY EXISTS IN 2024

Community Health Care Center Berlin:
The center is anchored in the neighborhood and offers a wide range of medical treatment and community services which are easily accessible, multilingual and free of cost.
▸ **geko-berlin.de**

Buurtzorg:
This is a pioneering healthcare organization established in 2006 that follows a nurse-led model of holistic care. It has revolutionized community care in the Netherlands.
▸ **buurtzorg.com**

→ to as "long-term" and "elder care." Most people who receive assistance in everyday life are also supported by the people close to them. This is possible because social security provisions mean that assistants are paid well and that people in need of help also receive it. The work of the assistants is held in high esteem in society, and the 20-hour working week has significantly reduced the burden placed on care workers. However, working times are still long enough for assistants to develop a caring relationship and to speak with the people that they help. Supervision and training are integral to this, and these changes have greatly improved the well-being of both the people providing and receiving assistance.

Dependence on support and assistance is no longer associated with financial hardship. Well-equipped specialized advisory and support services are firmly anchored in city districts and rural communities with the aim of providing people with the best possible level of care. This includes ensuring that people with impairments are empowered to participate in social, economic and political life as much as possible, and engage in activities that are important to them. The great increase in autonomy that many people with impairments have experienced has also been made possible due to the development of a new approach to urban development. Streets, residential buildings, buses, trains, many recreational areas – in fact, the entire urban infrastructure – has been redesigned to be barrier-free. People with impairments are included when developing technical devices to ensure that these are tailored to their needs and to provide them with greater autonomy. Consequently, care homes are no longer needed. People decide where they would like to live and whether they want to live with other people, in shared housing or on their own. Many projects have sprung up in cities and rural areas where people with impairments are well cared for, and where they remain part of public life – but live calmer, quieter lives together with other people.

Freedom of Movement

9

In 2048, there is:

↦ freedom of movement
↦ Welcome Centers
↦ Babelfish interpreters
↦ access to and participation
 in community resources

In 2048, there is no longer:

↤ border control
↤ deportations
↤ immigration authorities
↤ racism
↤ other forms of exclusion

Today, we all have the rights and opportunities to move freely, regardless of where we were born. Everyone has the same visa requirements. All passports provide the same benefits and we can travel without restrictive controls. Many people around the world are even campaigning for the complete abolition of passports and visas. No one has been deported since the late 2020s. The previous events when people were killed or left to die on the borders surrounding the Mediterranean Sea or North of Mexico are now considered crimes against humanity and warnings to the future.

2048

Former border area

Circular migration and Welcome Centres

✦ In the past, closed borders and unequal incomes resulted in migration mainly in one direction – this has changed fundamentally now that everyone has a chance to live a good life and that freedom of movement is guaranteed. Today, people move to other regions for a while – some stay, others move on, and others return. Circular migration is as normal now as it was in many areas of the world before the development of nation-states and colonialism. There is much more exchange among regions and cities all over the world.

There are Welcome Centers in every large neighborhood. These centers were established in old local authority offices and they include community cafés where people can meet. They are public institutions that do not sanction mobility but rather facilitate people arriving at new places. Welcome Centers are the first points of contact for new arrivals. They are places where people can meet and learn from one another, find host families and guest neighborhoods, and an overnight stay. They also offer Babelfish – computer-controlled headphones that provide interpreting and therefore aid with communication.

Nothing that people need to lead a good life – such as housing, education and health care – is linked to citizenship; rather, goods and services are made available to everyone who lives in a particular area. There is no discrimination: all forms of accommodation and neighborhoods are open to everyone, and everyone shapes the economy and labor. Appreciation of diversity and difference provides a basis for living together as a community.

Active against all forms of discrimination

⬤ Migration is no longer viewed as a problem, but rather as something completely normal. Everyone knows that we are all equally important. The vast majority of people have also torn down the borders in their minds and are actively ensuring that no forms of exclusion develop, such as stereotypes and prejudices based on racism, sexism, homophobia, transphobia, classism and the exclusion of people with disabilities. People actively counter the emergence of discrimination, exclusion and domination throughout society – in all institutions, in all relationships and on the streets.

Nobody is pigeonholed with questions such as "But where are you *originally* from?" or "Do you sell weed?" Stereotypes and prejudices are recognized as such and dealt with. Houses of Learning raise awareness about these issues and that everyone is responsible for ensuring that no one faces discrimination or exclusion within their daily lives, and people with privileges dismantle their privileges. In doing so, everyone learns the meaning of intersectionality – that is, how different forms of discrimination intertwine and how this leads to very specific experiences of discrimination.

Migration is the mother of all societies

⬤ Human history, as well as people's own histories, are told and shaped by everyone equally. People have learned to accept and expect diversity in public institutions and in all other areas of society; we value different languages, festivals, rituals and clothing styles. In fact, we believe that a variety of perspectives enriches society. The media no longer merely provides sensationalist reports about catastrophes, but instead engages in constructive journalism that demonstrates the positive and valuable sides of migration.

DO WE NEED BORDERS?

In discussions about migration, borders are often treated as natural, just and necessary. Societies, it is argued, must control who enters and leaves their territory. Next to outright racism and welfare chauvinism, this view is sometimes based on fear – fear of losing jobs, prosperity, traditions and ways of life. But borders are not natural, just or even necessary. Migration and exchange among different groups has taken place for as long as there have been people. Borders between states have a comparatively short history. Ultimately, they were introduced to defend the interests of certain privileged groups against supposed "others."

Borders are one of the most important means of maintaining inequality: Of all the factors that determine a person's chances in life, the passport they hold plays the most important role. Borders separate people who live in areas where the benefits of capitalist growth are accumulating from everyone else – the people at whose expense these benefits have been, and are being accumulated. Freedom of movement for all is, therefore, a fundamental tenet of global justice.

Borders for people are not even necessary – freedom of movement poses no danger to anyone. Moreover, it is unrealistic to assume that millions of people would suddenly leave their homes in a world characterized by much greater material equality. And even if they were to do so, this would not be a problem. Fears about being "inundated" by foreigners tend to not be based on well-founded concerns about a loss of identity, but on racist propaganda aimed at preventing certain people from moving to particular countries. Migration is not a danger – it is a boon for every society.

2024

Afrique-Europe-Interact:

people from Africa and Europe work as part of a network and combine the fight for freedom of movement (the right to leave) with the fight for self-determined development (the right to stay).

▸ **afrique-europe-interact.net**

Solidarity cities:

provide local services regardless of nationality.

▸ **solidaritycities.eu**

Black Lives Matter:

fights against racism, police violence and the prison-industrial complex, and develops the Vision for Black Lives, a wide-ranging visionary political platform that sets out numerous political demands.

▸ **m4bl.org**

Center for Intersectional Justice:

works against overlapping forms of structural inequality and discrimination and advocates an intersectional justice perspective.

▸ **intersectionaljustice.org**

Excerpt from an article
by Andry Rakotomalala, published in *Mahajanga News* on 28 April 2048, translated into English by Babelfish (version 11.04)

I still remember exactly what the woman in the Welcome Center in Cottbus said to me:

"Dear Mr. Rakotomalala, you come from one of the most beautiful places on earth, I really don't know what Lausitz has to offer you."

I told her about my interest in industrial culture and the transformation of the coal mining regions.

"You live in a beautiful place too,"

I told her. She smiled. She explained that I needed a visa, but that they would apply for one and that I could enter the country even before the paperwork had arrived.

"Perhaps visa requirements will be done away with soon anyway; nobody really sees the point of it all anymore."

She accompanied me from Cottbus to Welzow, where I was handed the keys to my house and, ultimately, to my new life. After I had eaten my first solyanka there, she said she wanted to show me something else. We cycled to Lake Sedlitz. As we sat there, I realized that I probably wouldn't be there forever, but that perhaps I'd stay longer than I had planned. After 15 years, I'm happy to be back in my old home, but I really miss the people of Lausitz.

From a travelogue

Food & Agriculture

10

In 2048, there is
↦ good food for all
↦ local value creation
↦ a circular economy
↦ diversity in manufacturing,
   particularly in farms and handicrafts

In 2048, there is no longer
↤ hunger
↤ food speculation
↤ dumping wages
↤ private land ownership
↤ industrial agriculture

Today, we all eat well. Our food is healthy, sustainably produced and is usually processed and distributed locally. Agriculture is based on the natural cycles of the environment, and our food is also varied and reflects our cultures. A radical redistribution of land and capital has led to a new principle of the commons. We know that we live off – and with – the land and we have a sense of connectedness with the natural environment. Agricultural work and all of the demands it places on us are considered essential, valuable and beautiful.

2048

Good food for everyone

◀ Food is no longer merely about efficiency: fresh food and staple foods are freely accessible, and everyone takes their time to eat. Locally organized supply chains – which are often run by the people who receive the food – facilitate access to food, for example through communal kitchens in people's homes, the Centers of Life in neighborhoods (▶ 11 Housing), or collective meals in the Houses of Learning (▶ 11 Housing) and in companies (▶ 5 Manufacturing and business). All food is distributed and used; nothing is thrown away. Protein requirements are mainly covered by vegetable protein. The consumption of meat and dairy products has fallen significantly, and the animal husbandry that continues is focused on protecting the environment and animal welfare. The remaining animal agriculture is now extensive, rather than intensive. All parts of the animals we rear are used ("nose to tail"); nothing is wasted. Cities and villages are "edible" because food is grown and harvested everywhere. Furthermore, because we understand that eating, growing and preparing food enriches our lives, we appreciate and revel in the chance to do so.

Diverse forms of working

Agriculture today reflects the principle of an all-round duty of care and diversity in farming. The focus is on small structures like farms and crafts. Smallholder structures are diverse: in addition to traditional family businesses, we have numerous agricultural enterprises run by extended families, collectives and cooperatives.

Agriculture is agroecological – in other words, it is focused on the long-term, being environmentally sustainable and mostly smallholder-based. Fossil-based or chemical fertilizers and pesticides are no longer used because they destroy environmental cycles. To produce all food organically, many more people have to work in agriculture than was the case at the beginning of the 21st century; however, agricultural workers now have good working conditions, more time to do their work and more contact with the recipients of their produce.

Producers largely run their own operations. Small-scale structures such as communal farm shops and distribution points, weekly markets and local processing chains have helped establish regional supply chains. Cooperative shops run by staff and consumers, and stocked with regional products, have replaced supermarkets run for profit. Our Community Centers (▶ 11 Housing) decide which producers they would like to work with and what they need. The decision by the Global Food Council to radically redistribute land and capital has led to a new principle of the commons because private land ownership has been abolished. Rules of use have been adopted by almost all regional councils (▶ 2 Democracy), and these rules are geared towards the long-term preservation of soil fertility. Most means of production in agriculture are also owned by local people but are networked globally. They are also jointly produced, used, repaired and developed (▶ 7 Technology). Everyone also has access to local seed centers, which are part of a network as well. The raw materials required for manufacturing are produced regionally and everyone has the opportunity to farm land.

Circular economy and soil conservation

We view every intermediate product – even every "waste product" – as a resource, which has enabled us to establish a truly circular economy. Even human feces can be composted with the right safety requirements – mixed sewage systems are therefore a thing of the past. This closes nutrient cycles and guarantees product standards so that compost remains safe and rich in nutrients.

We acknowledge the value of soil and focus on preserving and improving soil fertility. Our fields are smaller, and land is almost never left uncovered, thereby significantly reducing soil erosion. The build-up of humus makes an important contribution to high yield agroecological agriculture and the binding of greenhouse gases. Preserving and promoting biodiversity is a very important aspect of agriculture. Among other things, this means that artificial pesticides and herbicides are no longer used. At the same time, we have many more trees, hedges and niches for insects and wild animals, and farmers are growing old, non-hybrid and true-to-seed varieties of plants that they can propagate themselves. Agroforestry, permaculture and terra preta are all in use and have been further developed.

Specialized but re-localized distribution

Distribution and sales still require a large division of labor and specialization that involves a great deal of know-how. However, products no longer travel around the world from a farm to our plates; rather, they are largely processed and distributed locally.

A large proportion of our food is grown directly for particular neighborhoods without monetary remuneration. We have many small bakeries, butchers, mills, dairies and the like that operate as cooperatives and provide a well-selected range of high-quality stock originating within a 200-kilometer radius, wherever possible. Trade in products from the Global South such as coffee, tea and tropical fruit only takes place if food sovereignty and fair trade can be guaranteed at the cultivation sites. Children and young people learn to work with food at an early age and thus gain a natural connection to it. This also increases their interest in working in the food and agricultural sectors.

Weekly newsletter from Douarnenez Center of Life,
June 2049

Dear citizens of Douarnenez,

We're writing to tell you about the dishes that will be cooked and available in the Community Center this week, which you find below. But first, some more general information: On Monday, the House of Learning will be cooking for us with food from their learning garden. We can all look forward to early potatoes, spinach, aubergines and courgettes.

And speaking of early potatoes!

As you have noticed on the fields, it's harvest time, so the vanilla pudding collective and the Legrand family would really appreciate your help. Please put your name down at the Community Center or in the app if you can help with the harvest.

*We are expecting the first delivery from our **partner municipality Agrigento** in two weeks. We are all looking forward to olive oil and oranges!*

*The **mulch workshop** is currently understaffed until November and would appreciate one or two volunteers.*

Food available in the Community Center on Monday:

LUNCH — new potatoes with leafy spinach on a bed of fresh vegetables, with curd (vegan/vegetarian)
– vegetable seitan casserole
– vegan chocolate mousse

DINNER - gnocchi with tomato and mint sauce
- pearl barley stew with fresh bread
- apple puree with custard

As always, the Community Center is staffed from 8 am until 7 pm if you would like to pick up food to cook for yourself.

Enjoy your meal!

2024

WHAT ALREADY EXISTS IN 2024

Via Campesina:
fights throughout the world for self-determined smallholder organic agriculture.

▸ **viacampesina.org**

Community Supported Agriculture (CSA):
committed to the spread of solidarity-based agriculture.

▸ **communitysupportedagriculture.org.uk**

Nyéléni Network for Food Sovereignty:
a global food sovereignty network that builds on the 2007 Nyéléni Declaration.

▸ **nyeleni-eca.net**

Park Slope Food Coop:
long-standing cooperatively run food shop in New York

▸ **foodcoop.com**

Slow Food Youth:
global network of young people campaigning for good-quality, environmentally friendly, fairly traded food.

▸ **slowfoodyouthnetwork.org**

Animal Justice Project:
campaigns for the abolishment of animal exploitation and oppression.

▸ **animaljusticeproject.com**

WHY ISN'T THE FUTURE VEGAN?

In 2024, there were many debates about whether the future should be fully vegan – that is, free of animal products. Climate activists and leading scientists spoke in favor of a plant-based future because they viewed vegan small-scale farming as healthy both for people and the planet. However, the majority of the population viewed meat as part of their everyday diets.

Our Future Workshop on food made it clear that there must be an end to factory farming and that meat production – if it were to continue at all – must respect animal welfare. The question as to whether animals and meat can form part of sustainable agriculture was a contentious issue. Many arguments were put forward by all sides, and we pick up on a few of them here.

A key argument in favor of an animal food cycle is that in certain regions, it makes grasslands accessible, which can then be used to produce other food for people. Sustainable use of grassland helps preserve biodiversity while cooling the planet. Grass covers around 40% of the vegetated land surface worldwide and stores almost 50 percent more carbon in the soil below it than forest soils do. Grazing ruminants build up valuable fats and proteins from the grass – which is indigestible by humans, and at the same time produce manure – which can be used as fertilizer on the field to ensure long-term yields.

However, industrial agriculture is clearly nothing like this. Synthetic fertilizer is produced with a great deal of fossil energy and is spread on arable land to produce grain, corn and soy that is then fed to animals. This results in animal suffering and environmental destruction.

As stressed above, a new approach to agriculture and animal consumption is urgently needed because organic agriculture based on the natural cycles of the environment produces significantly smaller amounts of milk and meat. New methods of non-animal farming and horticulture must be developed – and some say, should even become dominant. However, for the time being, particularly from a global perspective, animals remain an essential part of a sustainable, organic agricultural cycle. Therefore, we stress the need for a fundamentally new approach to agriculture that does not rely exclusively on veganism.

Housing

11

In 2048, there is no longer:

⬅ homelessness

⬅ profits from property ownership

⬅ drab blocks of flats

⬅ anonymous neighborhoods

⬅ districts and villages that lack everyday necessities

Today we all live in lively neighborhoods based around a focal point that we call our Center of Life or Community Center. We live in different forms of accommodation and are able to decide where we would like to live. We can also adapt our accommodation to our needs as it is cooperatively run and community-owned. Climate-friendly lifestyles are not only possible but have even become completely normal. Life in the countryside is different from life in the city but just as attractive.

2048

Diverse forms of accommodation

Everyone can choose the type of accommodation that they would like to live in. Residential units are multifunctional and can be used for various activities. People live in different family forms – as (chosen) families, couples, in shared flats and accommodation that combines living areas with community spaces. When people enter a new phase of their life, it is not difficult to find a different place to live – and this means that people can live independently into old age. All forms of accommodation are legal; this includes moving into unused buildings, trailers, tents or converted trucks. Accommodation is no longer provided for profit. Land is publicly owned and managed by the community as a common good.

Community Centers

Living space is distributed relatively evenly: everyone has enough living space and more space that they can use than they did in the past. Although we now have less individual living space, more areas are used collectively. Ground floors of residential buildings in cities house solidarity-based, environmentally friendly enterprises or common rooms where we can meet one another (these spaces can also be in separate buildings).

Every neighborhood and village has a *Community Center* or *Center of Life*: a place where people can cook for each other, eat together, share ideas, distribute care work and welcome newcomers. We also share all the infrastructure that people need for a good life (e.g. washing areas, workshops, studios, playrooms, rehearsal rooms, sports halls, cinemas, media centers and gardens). These spaces are open and can be used in a variety of ways. Our society now has a greater feeling of togetherness and strong neighborhood solidarity. We also have Welcome Centers (▶ 9 Freedom of movement), Health Clinics (▶ 8 Health and participation) and Houses of Learning (▶ 14 Education); these may be shared by several districts.

Climate-friendly construction and building usage

Sam's daily life

🔵 All buildings are powered by 100% renewable energy. Plants grow on façades and roofs to regulate the local climate and provide space to grow food. Everyday necessities such as shops, playgrounds and Health Centers are within walking distance. This makes climate-friendly lifestyles not only possible, but also completely normal.

Our neighborhoods were created mainly through the sustainable conversion of existing buildings. These projects focused on the needs of residents and were implemented democratically. However, some new buildings were built as part of sustainable quarters. Only renewable, locally sourced and reused materials were used in construction.

Sam (born 2034): I live in the district of Lindenau in Leipzig. The place where we are now is very important to this area: It's our Community Center, which is basically the center of our lives. It provides food for everyone; people can come and pick up staple foods here. We also have a communal kitchen that provides delicious hot meals twice a day. New arrivals to our community come here too, because it also serves as our Welcome Center. I've probably met most of my best friends here. This is where our weekly neighborhood council meetings take place and it's where we decide how care work is shared among us. I learned how important it is for children to take care of the little ones from an early age. Apparently only girls used to be allowed to do this, which is why people thought it could be done better. I live around the corner in a large flat share. In our building there are many flats; most are different sizes, so people can move around as needed. A young family has just swapped with an older couple who lived with a good friend in a four-room flat.

How I live

Fair housing allocation and cost-based rent

● We use digital tools to organize, search for and allocate living spaces. Individuals, families and groups register their needs on an online portal that compares their needs to available accommodation. If several people would like to move into the same accommodation or district, lots are drawn. The data needed to run this system are well protected and publicly owned.

Tenants receive temporary usage rights, and accommodation cannot be privatized. Rents are charged, but these cover only the costs of maintenance and investment. Any surpluses are used to construct and convert further living spaces – this is similar to the way in which housing cooperatives operated in the past.

2024

An appealing life in the country

WHAT ALREADY EXISTS IN 2024

Expropriate Deutsche Wohnen:
aims to expropriate large housing corporations in Berlin to ensure that everyone can access good living spaces.

▸ dwenteignen.de/en

Mietshäuser Syndikat:
a network of housing cooperatives that has been permanently withdrawn housing from the housing market.

▸ syndikat.org/en

o500:
a model of an ideal district designed for 500 people.

▸ o500.org

Housing not profit – European Action Coalition for the Right to Housing and to the City:
brings movements together from different cities in several European countries that are fighting to ensure that the fundamental rights to housing and the city are respected.

▸ housingnotprofit.org

Radical Routes:
a network of radical (mostly housing) cooperatives that are committed to working for positive, radical social change.

▸ radicalroutes.org.uk

Because life in the country is more appealing than it was at the beginning of the century, young and active people are no longer leaving the countryside for the cities. All settlements and villages have everything that people need to enjoy everyday life, such as Community Centers (which provide people with everything that they need), Houses of Learning and Health Centers, with cafés, theatres, cinemas and much more, located in the center of larger villages. Village federations have been formed to jointly provide goods and services to smaller villages in places that are easy to reach via cycle paths and public transport. The commuting distances to paid employment are short when the type of work makes this possible (▸ 12 Mobility and transport).

Various forms of accommodation are available in the countryside. Detached homes for families with children have been redesigned to make good use of the space that becomes available when children move out. These buildings have been converted, transferred to other people, or are jointly used. Most buildings see mixed use or are used for co-working. In rural areas, too, Welcome Centers facilitate the arrival of new residents, and our villages and small towns are now much more diverse than they used to be (▸ 9 Freedom of movement).

Global connectedness

Even if society is focused on communities and neighborhoods – because this is where people put down roots and live out their daily lives – we address global developments and interconnectedness much more strongly than in the past. Information is freely accessible to all, and barriers such as language and the focus on written information are actively being broken down. People can move freely (▸ 9 Freedom of movement). Culture, dance, music and theatre are no longer produced and controlled by a small elite, but by everyone through the coexistence of different networked styles and traditions based around frequent contact.

Mobility & Transport

12

In 2048, there are:
- ↦ car-free towns and village squares
- ↦ appealing trains and stations
- ↦ a cargo bike decoration culture
- ↦ bike lanes and bike streets
- ↦ well-timed, regular public transport, including bicycle taxis

In 2048, there is no longer:
- ↤ unnecessary transport aimed at benefitting from cost advantages
- ↤ motorways
- ↤ mass tourism
- ↤ short-haul flights
- ↤ other forms of fossil-fuelled mobility

Although there is much less traffic today, we are more mobile than people were in the past. Instead of a culture of acceleration and infrastructure aimed at encouraging fast individual transport, we created a world of short distances which we bridge using environmentally friendly means of transport that are accessible to everyone.

2048

Mobility in the countryside

Rural areas now have far less need for transport than in the past. This is because:

→ All settlements and villages now have everything they need for a good life (▸ 11 Housing).

→ The economic focus lies on care work, which is also needed in villages (▸ 8 Health and participation)

→ The re-regionalization of handicrafts, manufacturing and other production sites means that most people can now work close to where they live.

→ Food provision has been decentralized and is provided by smallholder agriculture (▸ 10 Food and agriculture).

→ The establishment of co-working spaces that allow people to participate in transregional projects without feeling isolated and to share technology to save resources.

Many more people now live and work in the countryside, and they are no longer forced to commute to cities.

→

Mobility in the city

→ Services for everyday life are so close by that they can be reached by bike or free public transport. The synchronization of working hours in sparsely populated areas also means that local public transport is well utilized. People who find it difficult to get around use (bicycle) taxis to cover the last stretch; these are available in every village or network of villages.

Village squares are often car-free. To get to the next village or town, some people still use small electric cars, but they usually share them. Ride-sharing benches (which are everywhere), the deceleration of everyday life and the elimination of discrimination have made hitchhiking appealing again. At the same time, well-developed bicycle lanes have been built between communities, and many shops, bicycle self-help workshops and other businesses have sprung up close to them in response. These are separated by small quiet areas and gardens.

A culture of sharing, Community Centers (▸ 11 Housing), urban gardening and open workshops have greatly reduced traffic in the city. Just as in the rural areas, people find everything that they need for their everyday lives in their immediate vicinity, and the goods and services they need may even be produced locally.

Except for the vehicles needed to transport particularly heavy items (e.g. refuse or building materials) and emergency vehicles, most cities are car-free. And even the numbers of emergency vehicles have declined because people have far fewer traffic accidents. As a result, urban spaces have become safe places for everyone to engage in conversation, play, and to enjoy peace and quiet. Streets have been replaced by bike lanes (often divided into fast lanes and normal lanes), parks, small green spaces, flowerbeds, playgrounds and much more. There are fewer differences between cities and countryside now, so city-dwellers have less need to go "relax in the countryside." People tend to use free public transport for long distances, and bicycle (taxis) for shorter distances.

PASSENGER PICK-UP

SHARE IT
HALLEIPZIG

Long-distance transport and travel

Motorways have been replaced by single-lane roads with a speed limit of 100 km/h that are mainly used by electric buses as well as a few trucks and smaller vehicles. In contrast, the length of the rail network hast doubled while train employees have tripled, many of which are former employees of the automotive, heavy and fossil fuel industry. For longer distances the train is the default, since it is the most comfortable, fastest and cheapest option.

Travelling by train has changed a great deal since the early years of the 21st century. Train stations now combine mobility centers with meeting places, cozy open kitchens, lounges, sleeping areas, reading corners and relaxation rooms. The trains themselves have themed compartments, provide care and entertainment for children, and are very comfortable. The latter is especially true for the large international network of night trains. The speed of trains has been limited to a maximum of 200 km/h, which reduces energy consumption and means that the tracks can be less straight. The trains run entirely on renewable energy – a small part of which is even produced in the trains' own fitness room by harnessing the exertions of passengers during the journey.

Due to the deceleration of everyday life and the reduction in working hours, short trips by plane are a thing of the past. In general, the need for holidays to escape the stresses of everyday life has decreased significantly. Instead, we usually travel for longer periods – either for a few weeks by train or electric barge, or take even more distant trips by night train or solar sailing ship. Many people take several months off to do so. Because everyday life is less stressful, we do not use these trips to recover as much as possible in the shortest possible time, but instead take our time to get to know other ways of life, landscapes and regions.

We still have planes and airports, but we now consider them to be much less appealing than people did in the past. Unlike train stations, the few airports that do still exist are purely functional. Aviation is mainly used by people who need to travel quickly – especially people who need to flee their country quickly or whose families are difficult to reach by ship. These days, we have hardly any intra-European flights, and no one flies without a real need because flying is expensive, uncomfortable and widely viewed as irresponsible.

Freight transport

The regionalisation of economic cycles has greatly reduced cross-regional freight transport in most regions (▶ 1 Global Justice). In some areas, however, long-distance transport is used, but it is designed to be efficient. Even in these cases, we no longer transport raw materials or unprocessed foods over long distances. Instead, the processing takes place at the local level and the products are then transported by solar sailing ships and trains. At the local level, many items are transported by cargo bike. In fact, a whole tradition of decorated cargo bikes has arisen around these means of transport, based on the way in which vehicles are painted in South Asia.

BUT WHERE ARE ALL THE AUTONOMOUS ELECTRIC VEHICLES?

Electromobility plays a major role in most future transport scenarios. The aim is not just to promote climate-friendly forms of public transport, but also to maintain today's car-focused lifestyle. However, this also means retaining all of its negative consequences – accidents, surface sealing, noise, as well as resource and energy consumption. That is why we consider this to be a flawed approach. Autonomous vehicles are also a hot topic when it comes to issues of future mobility. Proponents claim that these vehicles would significantly reduce accidents, traffic jams and energy consumption if they were to be effectively used as public vehicles. However, we see very little need for autonomous vehicles because cars of any type play only a very limited role in our vision, and because there are many persuasive arguments against them. Autonomous vehicles, could, for example make driving more appealing and encourage more people to drive longer distances. Additionally, they also require resource-intensive information processing infrastructures that generate huge amounts of data and are questionable from a data protection perspective.

2024

WHAT ALREADY EXISTS IN 2024

1000s of organizations:
fighting for environmentally friendly traffic in their neighborhood, village, city and country.

‣ changing-cities.org

‣ einsteigen.jetzt

‣ rothe-ecke.de

‣ systemchange-not-climatechange.at

‣ wanderbaumallee-stuttgart.de

Initiatives in Notre-Dame-des-Landes, London and Munich:
successfully resisting airport construction (and expansion).

‣ wikipedia.org/wiki/ZAD_de_Notre-Dame-des-Landes

‣ airportwatch.org.uk

‣ keine-startbahn3.de

GroenLinks:
the Dutch political party calling for flights under 750 km to be banned.

‣ back-on-track.eu/groenlinks-uk

Sailcargo:
a company that builds cargo sailing ships.

‣ sailcargo.org

Austrian Federal Railways:
a company that is expanding the European night train network.

‣ nightjet.com

Climate perks:
some companies now offer their staff more holiday time if they do not fly.

‣ climateperks.com

Stay Grounded:
works on a global level to reduce air traffic and build a climate-just transport system.

‣ stay-grounded.org

News from Annaba
Date: 20 June 2048
From Katia, to Maik

Hello, Maik! We've arrived in Annaba!

We travelled again by night train, sailing ship and bus, and everything went well. The only exciting thing that happened was that I was finally allowed to set the sails of the ship myself and to go up into the crow's nest. And you won't believe it! Remember Urtan (the son of our host family, who used to be really annoying)? He's completely different. Last year he hung out with my mum and his dad whenever they were talking about desalination systems. But this year we are getting on really well and he wants to show me how to windsurf. Tomorrow we're going to Lake Fetzara with the Hamadis for a week. They organized a bike bus and Urtan is going to help me with my Arabic on the trip. I hope you have a great time in Tbilisi – see you in about 50 days!

Love, Katia.

Email from holiday

In 2048, there are:

↦ Energy-sufficient lifestyles
↦ the 1250-Watt Society
↦ an International Climate Council
↦ democratically and locally
  planned energy provision

In 2048, there are no longer:

↤ CO_2 emissions from the
  production of electricity
↤ transport or heating sectors
↤ an energy or industry lobby
↤ a profit-based energy sector

Today we produce and consume much less than 30 years ago. We also show far more appreciation of things that have grown or aged naturally. Life runs at a slower pace, and we acknowledge that we are part of the natural world, which in turn results in a responsible use of resources and lifestyles based on sufficiency.

2048

Energy consumption

▲ The 1250-Watt Society is based on the idea of a 2000-Watt Society that first arose in Switzerland 30 years ago. Today, no one uses on average more than 1250 watts of primary energy (10950 kWh per year). This is about a quarter of the energy that people consumed in 2020. Our neighborhood structures provide numerous ways to fulfil your need for entertainment that use very little energy (▸ 11 Housing) while the energy we need to cover our basic needs (mobility, heat and light) is provided as part of basic services.

Energy supply

Due to global warming, humanity had to act urgently and change the way that we produced and used energy. As such, we have greatly reduced our energy consumption compared to the 2030s, and our energy needs are now completely met by renewables. In the electricity-sector, long-established and resource-saving technologies such as photovoltaic cells, wind turbines and power storage systems have evolved, simplifying the balancing of production and consumption.

We have significantly lowered everyone's heating requirements by reducing the size of living spaces and by using modern forms of insulation (based on environmentally friendly insulation materials). Wherever possible, our remaining energy requirements are now covered by simpler resource-saving technologies such as solar thermal and geothermal energy.

Energy consumption has also fallen sharply in the transport sector because mobility is no longer based around cars and planes (▶ 12 Mobility and transport). All remaining motorized vehicles are now powered by electricity from renewable sources.

Energy distribution is regionally diverse. In some regions, self-sufficient neighborhoods are the rule while others rely on local grids or even the old, but well-maintained power grids spanning greater areas.

The technical side of energy supply is organized by "e-nerd collectives" (energy service providers). These diverse groups consist of people who are interested in power generation and learn from one another. They are responsible for a region's energy supply, i.e. building and repairing wind turbines, photovoltaic panels and electricity grids.

The supply and distribution of energy is now publicly controlled and democratically planned at the local level (▶ 2 Democracy).

Beginner's level:
the Global Climate Council
Last updated 5 December 2048

In the past, climate negotiations involved meetings between countries that were primarily in economic competition with one another. These countries had ulterior motives to which a joint effort to stop global warming was secondary – as a result, climate negotiations were characterized by tactical maneuvers. The voluntary government commitments that resulted failed to reduce global emissions. Most societies transitioned to a cooperative, needs-based economy after the 2028 crisis and therefore no longer compete with one another. Nevertheless, we still need a global planning level today to:

→ ensure that we remain on a climate-friendly path at the global level;

→ decide how to distribute resources that are available locally but needed globally, such as rare earth metals; and

→ plan a global recycling regime.

These tasks are assumed by the Global Climate Council, which is representative in terms of people's origin and of minorities. It tends to act in an advisory capacity while considering the historical guilt of the countries of the Global North (the industrialized countries contributed much more to global warming). The work of the council benefits from the fact that almost all regions are pursuing the same goal: ending global warming. However, if a region were to miss its reduction targets, the Council can impose sanctions, but these must not affect the goods and services that people need for their everyday lives.

Learning Wiki

2024

WHAT ALREADY EXISTS IN 2024

International organizations like Greenpeace, 350.org and Powershift: organize protests and non-violent direct action against fossil fuels and nuclear power. They are supported by many smaller organizations...

▸ greenpeace.org

▸ 350.org

▸ powershift.org

School pupils from Fridays for Future: strike for climate justice.

▸ fridaysforfuture.org

Energy cooperatives: promote the energy transition from the ground up.

▸ rescoop.eu

Climate camps: demonstrate alternative ways of producing energy, provide space to learn and share experiences, and organize action against fossil fuels throughout the world.

▸ climatecampscotland.com

Climate policy

▲ Once we replaced rivalry and competition with cooperation and solidarity, we were able to use energy councils to develop effective climate policy structures. The councils discuss energy requirements and work out how much time, resources and pollution will be necessary to meet people's energy requirements. Finally, a joint decision is made as to whether the ends justify the means. Energy councils send representatives to higher-level councils, and the global level is organized by the Global Climate Council (see box).

Message to Historix Jorge Sczechuan
Quantum Transmission 3.48637KJ

Date: 23 May 4021

Hi Jorge, I read with interest your article on global warming in the 20th and 21st centuries. However, I tend to disagree with your conclusions. The dendrochronological analyses clearly demonstrate that atmospheric CO_2 was decreasing before the coal reserves available at the time were exhausted. Of course, we can only speculate as to whether mining was halted due to a positive policy decision or due to more primitive reasons such as "costs." Pollen analyses also suggest that a rapid and comprehensive rethinking took place, given that tree pollen diversity increased sharply at the end of the 2030s whereas monocultural finds throughout South America decreased. I therefore continue to maintain that the Century of Solidarity began before this period and can even be said to have started with the Environmental Policy Turn.

Message from the year 4021

Education

14

In 2048, there are:

↦ Houses of Learning
↦ life-long learning
↦ self-determined and
   interest-based learning
↦ cooperative group learning
↦ accompanied learning
↦ district, municipality and the world
   as places of learning

In 2048, there are no longer:

↤ Schools
↤ teaching
↤ learning directed by other people
↤ pressure to meet targets
↤ grades, tests, competition
↤ selection and division

Today we learn in open educational landscapes that encourage people of all ages to pursue their interests. We shape our own learning paths and are supported by learning companions. We have open, democratically organized Houses of Learning that provide space to meet, learn and to reflect. But the forest, the bicycle workshop and the neighborhood council – even those on the other side of the world – can also be part of our learning landscape. In addition to cultural techniques such as reading and writing, we gain practical experience that provides us with the basic skills we all need to live together in a sustainable and solidarity-based (world) society.

2048

Learning that develops people's potential

Education supports people in developing diverse skills and their own potential; it also enables them to face up to the demands imposed by life, living together and securing a livelihood. To preserve life on this planet, education is more strongly based on values such as human rights, children's rights and environmental rights than it was in the past, and these values have been agreed upon on at the global level. Open Houses of Learning help people acquire ways of being, and the skills as well as the knowledge they need to shape a sustainable, solidarity-based and peaceful society.

The learning cultures put in place in the various practical and theoretically based places of learning provide what we view as successful learning: recognition, healthy relationships, participation, responsibility and purpose. People learn by working with others to solve what they see as interesting problems, tasks and challenges. As such, we largely shape our own learning paths. People of all ages come together in the Houses of Learning in different groups (these may be based on interest or age) to organize and reflect on their own learning. Learners choose who they would like to learn with as well as who should help them reflect on what they have learned and provide facilitation, inspiration and advice.

The Houses of Learning offer diverse educational paths that appeal to different types of learners and provide the basic cultural techniques that people need →

to fully participate in society. These include opportunities to learn reading, writing and arithmetic, but also to practice problem-solving skills, critical thinking, openness, imagination and creativity, empathy and conflict-solving skills, teamwork, the courage to act and adopt responsibility, as well as the skills to deal with uncertainty when confronted with issues we do not yet understand.

Life itself offers the best learning opportunities. The local educational places network between spaces where people learn, live and try out practical activities. This brings together forests, workshops, laboratories, planning offices, health centers, farms, urban gardens, theatres and parliaments to form part of the educational landscape. These locations offer an aesthetic (hands-on, sensuous) way of discovering the world. People with the necessary pedagogical skills take time to mentor others as they learn theory and test their knowledge and skills. Learners contribute to solving real problems; they also come to understand that they can have an impact on society and that they need to adopt responsibility for shaping their shared environment. Numerous places of learning are globally networked and bring together people from different parts of the world to work on joint projects. Action and reflection are linked, because after a period of exploration and practice, learners come together in the Houses of Learning to share their experiences. They consider what they have learned, learn from one another, and plan how to implement what they have learned or set additional learning goals.

The error-friendly learning approach treats both success and failure as contributing to learning. We do not use grades and tests to monitor and compare learners; rather, we provide appreciative, voluntary feedback that is focused on a person's potential, in addition to self-evaluated learning processes. Instead of degrees, we follow educational paths full of new beginnings. If people want to learn more about a specific field or take a more in-depth educational path, they receive the support they need to do so from learning companions in the Houses of Learning. Companies and specialized training centers also draw up specialist entry requirements, which learners can use to focus their learning.

2024

Learning spaces of inclusion and equality

Like other social infrastructure, education is free of charge and accessible to everyone for life. The Houses of Learning are barrier-free and designed to meet people's needs. They are places where we learn to live together. Through the integration of diverse populations within neighborhoods, there is also a representation of the diverse perspectives and life situations of people in our society among the learners in the houses of learning. (▸ 11 Housing, ▸ 9 Freedom of movement). Different needs, such as different languages, are addressed flexibly. The learning companions also have diverse backgrounds. People of different origins, gender identities, physical abilities and ages are always part of the team. The teams also include people from various professions that have different experiences – such as educators, speech therapists, social workers, psychologists and physicists. The learning companions regularly take part in further training, consultations and facilitated meetings that provide a critical approach to power and hierarchy to reflect on the power expressed through their work and inherent within their own roles. Despite all our efforts, centuries-old forms of discrimination have yet to be completely eliminated; therefore, contact structures as well as empowerment and reflection rooms are made available in the Houses of Learning. They are shaped and used by people who experience discrimination as much as by those who experience privilege to work jointly towards a fair and just society.

Learning spaces of democracy

The Houses of Learning are places of democratic self-determination and self-government. The grassroots-democratic aspects of these institutions provide everyone with the opportunity to shape social relations, change situations and develop solutions that are acceptable to everyone. They also fully implement the Convention on the Rights of the Child. Children and young people can play an active role. In this way, everyone develops the courage, creativity and competences they need in today's society and can shape the present with a view to the future. Good education for everyone is of great importance to society, and sufficient public funds are made available for this purpose. The Council for Further Development provides the educational policy framework for educational experts, experts from all other areas of society, and learners from the Houses of Learning to define the shape of sustainable education. The goals of sustainable education have been drawn up by globally agreed frameworks, and they are implemented in the Houses of Learning. The Council for Further Development provides advice to the regional educational councils. In turn, the councils advise the independent Houses of Learning and coordinate and support networking and cooperation between the various educational landscapes.

Excerpt from a conversation between Josepha (mentor) and R'anja (learner)

R'anja: I just don't think it's right for me.

Josepha: Well, what about the Tech Collective?

R: I want to be an artist. I don't want to build things!

J: But lots of artists build things – sculptures, buildings – or they design things around us. And I think your strength lies in finding good technical solutions to problems. Do you remember when you designed that model of a music player? Even the nerds from the collective thought it was great.

R: But that was just a gimmick. I want to create something on canvas, a picture!

J: If that's important to you, then you need to go to a place for learning the arts.

R: But I don't want to leave this area.

J: Have you ever thought about taking an online course?

R: Do you think they really work? They're not the same as in-person courses.

J: No, they're not, but they are a good way of finding out whether you might enjoy doing art in the long term.

R: Okay, but then I won't have any more time for the metalworking shop!

J: No problem. But you know the rules: make sure you let the others know!

Finance

15

In 2048, there are:

↦ democratic banks

↦ democratically controlled money

↦ a Global Clearing Union for currencies

In 2048, there are no longer:

← financial, currency and banking crises

← floating exchange rates

← financial and currency speculation

Small, simple and focused on people's needs: The financial system

Markets and money play only a small role in everyday (business) life. Therefore, the financial system only plays a subordinate role in society. There is no need for many of the services that were provided by the financial system in the past, such as insurance – from private pensions to accident, disability, life and liability insurance. Everyone now has lifelong access to common infrastructure and social resources (▶ 4 Social security). Everyone owns more or less the same amount, so the financial system is quite limited. Since money can be inherited only in small amounts, most goods (e.g. living space) are managed as commons, with the maximum income significantly limiting the accumulation of assets (▶ 5 Manufacturing and business).

In the past, the financial system also mediated decisions about important investments in future infrastructure, research and product development. Today, however, these decisions are generally made by democratic institutions consisting of representatives from the respective economic sectors. And because joint stock companies, stock exchange, and highly complex financial instruments simply do not exist – in fact, no speculation at all – large sectors of the financial industry have simply disappeared.

Today's financial system has shrunk and has been radically simplified to a small core that is committed to the common good and placed under democratic regulation. It is possible to accumulate or inherit only a very limited amount of money. Despite this, we still have numerous financial institutions. However, banks, money and financial cooperatives no longer act as an independent system, but instead are tools placed at the disposal of a democratic society.

2048

Banks

The landscape of financial institutions in 2048 is diverse, consisting of small and medium-sized public banks, cooperatives and banks focused on the common good. Private and profit-oriented banks no longer exist; these fell into disrepute by the beginning of the 21st century, and only banks working toward the common good are allowed to operate. These institutions are strictly regulated and must follow democratically established criteria to ensure compliance with societal and environmental frameworks.

The financial system as a whole is geared to people's needs and to meeting social-environmental goals. Private financial institutions must bear the risks of their own operations. To minimize risk, basic services such as housing, mobility and food can be funded only by cooperatives or through public financing. However, private financing is available in less vital areas (such as consumer goods production, particularly lavish sporting events, and the like).

Everyone has access to all these financial institutions, which provide extensive opportunities for participation – not only to staff but also to account holders. Bank transfers are free for everyone; they take place in real time and via encrypted digital technologies. At the same time, a high level of data protection is necessary for the payment system, and payment information is only released to public institutions in exceptional cases.

WHY ISN'T OUR UTOPIA MONEY-FREE?

Discussions about money often become quite emotional. Some people consider money to be the root of all evil; others view it as a practical, neutral medium for exchange; and still others reject the market economy entirely. These arguments are often superimposed by the fact that criticisms of money and interest are often intertwined with anti-Semitic narratives.

During the development of this vision of the future, discussions about the (non)sense of money cropped up many times. We decided not to opt for a money-free vision for various reasons: first, our vision is clearly not an endpoint or a utopia; rather, it describes a transitional phase that must inevitably contain certain contradictions. Therefore, we decided that money should still exist, but that its role in society would be much reduced. Moreover, in the vision, money is aimed at satisfying people's needs and under democratic control. At the same time, however, we also describe aspects of society that go beyond market exchanges and thus work very well without money (▶ 3 Economy).

Overall, the importance of money and everything related to it (e.g. wage labor, exchange logic, taxes) steadily decreases between 2024 and 2048. At the same time, the importance of money-free forms of social and community cooperation has increased continuously. This process has not been completed by 2048, but in our vision, people are able to decide in which areas of social life and how much space they want money to take up in their lives – people in different places come to quite different conclusions. The main difference between 2024 and 2048, therefore, is that markets and money no longer determine how people live; rather, it is people who determine whether and how money and markets are to be used.

Where does the money go, and who makes the decisions?

Money, which is mainly available in electronic form, is created directly by a region's democratic and public central bank as "digital cash" and passed on to the various banks and to society directly via the various democratic economic institutions (▸ 2 Democracy, ▸ 3 Economy). The central bank is democratically controlled, but it retains a degree of independence to ensure that its policies focus on people's long-term well-being. All positions rotate, and its work is accountable and transparent. The payment system is public and secure – there has not been a major wave of bankruptcies since the great banking and financial crisis of the late 2020s.

In some areas, the public sector directly finances necessary and forward-looking investments and expenditures. For example, municipal health cooperatives invest transnationally in collaborative research on antibiotics. In other areas, democratic credit steering is used to secure finances for essential tasks. For example, European finance councils defined criteria in the 2020s that made it possible to finance the construction of the post-fossil energy supply (▸ The transformation). The banks and finance cooperatives took over democratic control of investment and lending in order to strengthen the development of a decentralized, resilient and subsidiary economy. The core task of banks is managing and wisely investing people's savings; they cannot create money themselves.

In addition to a global currency in which supra-regional transactions are processed, there are also self-owned, democratic, regional, complementary currencies that are focused on specific local circuits. Some people and districts operate local exchange trading systems. And, of course, a lot just happens without involving money at all. For many people, gift economies are an important part of their involvement in society; they work on projects that they view as useful and meaningful, and in turn are provided with goods and services that other people produce or offer (▸ 3 Economy).

2024

WHAT ALREADY EXISTS IN 2024

Attac:
the network exists in many countries and uses education, campaigns, direct actions and demonstrations to call for a fundamental re-regulation of the financial system and a socio-ecological transformation.

▸ **attac.org**

Finance Watch:
fights against the influence of the financial lobby and to have the financial industry placed at the service of society.

▸ **finance-watch.org**

Jubilee Debt Campaign:
campaigns to ensure that the living conditions of people in indebted countries are prioritized over the repayment of national debts.

▸ **jubileedebt.org.uk**

Debt for Climate:
a global grassroots movement initiated and led by the Global South, building power from the bottom-up to cancel the financial debt of the Global South in order to enable a self-determined, just transition.

▸ **debtforclimate.org**

Positive Money:
campaign for a money and banking system that enables a fair, sustainable and democratic economy.

▸ **positivemoney.org**

A Global Clearing Union for currencies

A Global Clearing Union has been established between currency areas. It uses fixed exchange rates and an international clearing currency to ensure that surpluses and deficits among currency areas can be solved cooperatively and to avoid critical imbalances.

The main aim is to harmonize and raise living standards globally within ecological limits. During the 2020s, this included international debt relief for countries in the Global South. Additionally, the union aims to promote economic subsidiarity and stability – which also means that currency areas export roughly as much as they import. Regions may temporarily introduce capital controls if necessary. Due to strict upper limits on currency ownership, there is no speculation on foreign exchange, which, in the past, often led to catastrophic crises.

How do we get there?

▶ When envisioning transformative futures, we face two important questions. The first is easier to answer: *What kind of society do we want to live in?* The second is far more daunting: *What do we need to do to create that society?* For a society such as the one we have outlined here to develop, so much would have to change in almost all areas of life, and at almost all levels. It is hard to imagine what such transformative developments would look like. More importantly, this is a question of social power. Some people believe that there is no need to make such changes – and others would even attempt to prevent them because they benefit from today's society and its power structures (or believe they do). Crucially, those who would benefit most from a more equitable social, political and economic order tend to have less power to force through such changes. These points become particularly clear when enormous levels of resistance are expressed, even against relatively small changes such as introducing universal health care in the US, allowing uncensored internet access in China or phasing out coal in Germany.

In many places, there is no political (party) majority or social movement strong enough to push through the fundamental changes that are presented in this vision. But it does not have to remain that way!

The transformation

People write history

▶ People make history, and they do so within the social conditions they encounter. Societies change; existing power structures can be transformed or torn down and rebuilt. Things that previously seemed unimaginable can become possible. Sometimes, crises accelerate change, and we can never really know where that change will take us.

Even if our project focuses on the question of what a *Future for All* might look like, we used our *Future Workshops* to discuss detailed paths that could lead to this vision. In the following, we draw on some insights from these debates. However, like everything else in this vision, what follows is an invitation for broadening imaginations and critical discussions aimed at encouraging further development. Although nobody knows how such a transformation might take place, it is up to us all to make it happen.

How do societies change?

▶ Social change is driven by many different people, organizations and networks pursuing different strategies and interests simultaneously. This is clear from historical studies on the abolition of slavery, the introduction of women's suffrage and the possibilities of implementing utopias (see box). Social change is not driven only by politics: it can also be driven by people in social movements as well as the media, pioneers, consumers, scientists, unions, parents, artists, teachers, school pupils – that is, by all of us. Fundamental change becomes possible when people organize collectively and many different actors work in the same direction. In doing so, different strategies must complement one another. Following the sociologist and transformation researcher Erik Olin Wright, we consider three strategies to be central to social change.

The first strategy involves people outside of the market and the state experimenting with different institutions, infrastructures and forms of organization. These interstitial spaces – from community supported agriculture to self-run nurseries and cooperatives – are laboratories in which other forms of economic relationships and coexistence are tested. They emerge within – and despite – the old structures, and they anticipate a sustainable social system on a small scale. Such "nowtopias" change people and their desires, constitute spaces of learning and, in combination with other strategies, can result in qualitative changes to social systems.

The second strategy focuses on today's structures, institutions and laws, and seeks to implement →

successive change through radical but symbiotic reforms. Political reforms that go beyond the current social system to promote further transformation beyond capitalism have been theorized by Rosa Luxemburg as "revolutionary realpolitik." This includes policies such as reducing working hours, introducing maximum incomes, ecological reparations, radically redistributing income and wealth, improving community participation and providing a basic income.

The third strategy is that of building counter-hegemonic power through ruptures. The development of other economic structures from below and achieving fundamental reforms requires not only political majorities, but also the necessary means, resources and social power to push through such changes. Fundamental social change is only possible if various actors – from the media to political parties and economic pioneers – come together to forge forward-looking alliances to shift discourses. In other words, they spread a worldview that stands for a future for all and that goes beyond current power relations to fight together for an inclusive, feminist, anti-racist, decolonial, environmental, democratic and accessible society. People must think about these issues themselves and as part of their personal relationships, on the streets, in factories, hospitals and parliaments. We need mass strikes, political parties and unions – but also more radical actions such as mass civil disobedience.

All these strategies must focus on the social developments that are taking place at the current time; these are often accompanied – or caused – by crises. As we mentioned in the introduction, the COVID-19 pandemic demonstrates just how deeply crises can transform societies, and that they can also provide windows of opportunity for a future for all – if only we are ready to seize them.

LITERATURE ON SOCIAL TRANSFORMATION

Akuno, Kali/Nangwaya, Ajamu: **Jackson Rising: The Struggle for Economic Democracy and Black Self-Determination in Jackson, Mississippi**. Ottawa: Daraja Press, 2017.

Bajpai,Shrishtee/Friess, Susanne/Kothari, Ashish/Kuhnhenn, Kai/Mabanza Bambu, Boniface and Treu, Nina. **Towards a socio-ecological transformation of the economy. An overview of concepts, approaches and practices**. Misereor, 2024.

Bevins, Vincent. **If We Burn: The Mass Protest Decade and the Missing Revolution**. New York: PublicAffairs, 2023.

Bollier, David, and Silke Helfrich. **Free, Fair, and Alive: The Insurgent Power of the Commons**. Gabriola Island, Canada: New Society Publishers, 2019.

Engler, Mark, and Paul Engler. **This Is an Uprising: How Nonviolent Revolt Is Shaping the Twenty-First Century**. Public Affairs, 2016.

Jackson, Tim. **Post Growth—Life after capitalism**. Cambridge: Polity Press, March 2021.

Luxemburg, Rosa. **The Mass Strike, the Political Party and the Trade Unions**. Berlin: Manifest, 1906.

Polanyi, Karl. **The Great Transformation: The Political and Economic Origins of Our Time.** Boston: Beacon Press, 2002.

Kothari, Ashish/ Salleh, Ariel/ Escobar, Arturo/ Demaria, Federico and Acosta, Alberto (Editors). **Pluriverse: A Post-Development Dictionary**. Delhi: Authors Up Front, 2019.

Scheidler, Fabian. **The End of the Megamachine: A Brief History of a Failing Civilisation**. Zer0 books: 2020.

Schmelzer, Matthias/ Vansintjan, Aaron and Vetter, Andrea. **The Future Is Degrowth: A Guide to a World Beyond Capitalism**. London: Verso, 2022.

Wright, Erik Olin. **Envisioning Real Utopias**. New York: Verso, 2010.

The Megatrends

In our vision, social change could come about due to the influence of five "megatrends" that depend on – and influence – one another, and are therefore intertwined. These are described in more detail in the following report from the future.

2024

Finance

Fifty-eight daily newspapers around the world report on the biggest financial scandal in history; it was uncovered by a whistle-blower who used to be a financial lobbyist. The worldwide outrage leads to a growing movement, more awareness among the population, reforms on lobbying and tighter regulation.

Housing

The Deutsche Wohnen real estate group in Berlin is expropriated, setting a precedent for other cities. London, Frankfurt, New York and Jakarta soon follow suit.

Food & Agriculture

Community organizing is used in the agricultural sector, bringing together farmers, social movements and local populations all over Europe. They organize (among other things) cooking protests against food waste, public snacks and trips to food producers. They also launch a popular podcast.

2025

Technology

Inspired by climate action and further catalyzed by the COVID-19 pandemic, hackers develop a digital protest form: "No Platform Friday" which puts pressure on digital media for more data protection and advertising bans.

Economy

Social Security

An unconditional basic income is introduced in three European regions as well as New Zealand, following the example of Taiwan. A comprehensive study five years later concludes that in 90% of cases it improved people's lives. Australia, Canada and the other European countries follow suit in introducing an AUB.

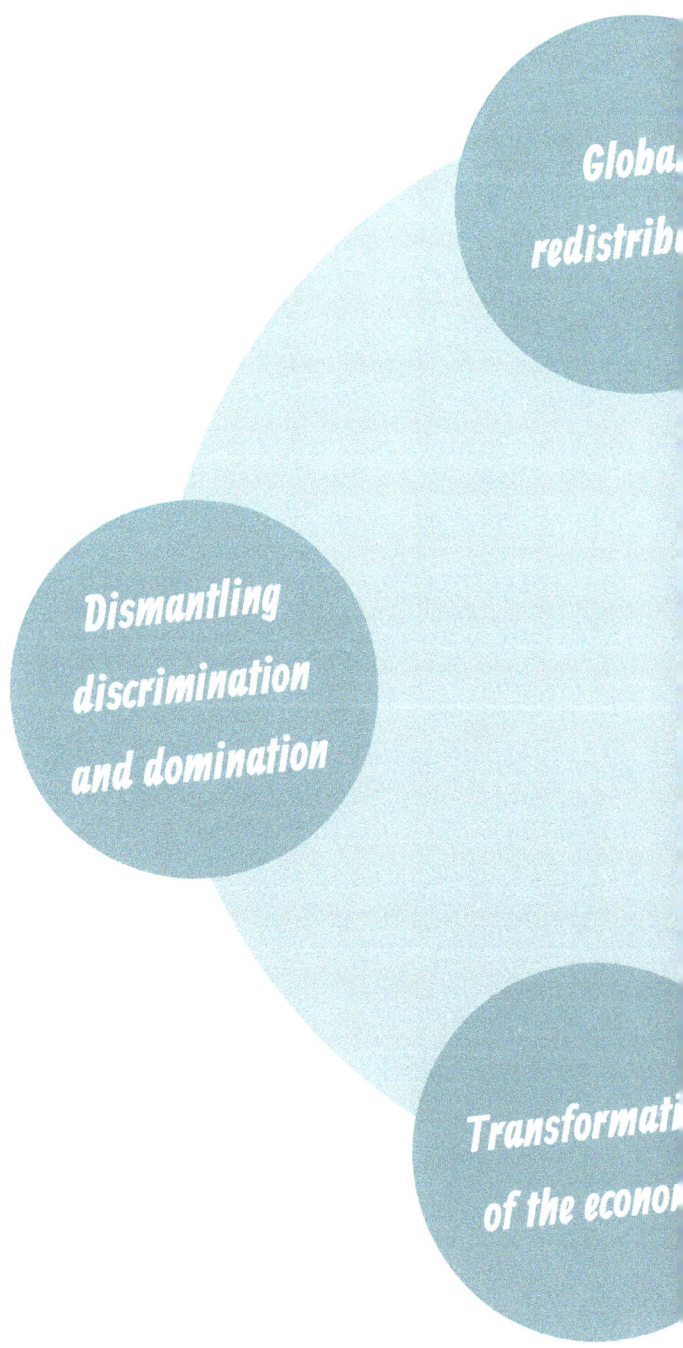

Global redistribu

Dismantling discrimination and domination

Transformati of the econom

Assuming that social developments follow the best possible direction: How did we get from the 2020s to a Future for All in 2048?

Environmental transformation

Self-determination and democratization

Through representatives of the degrowth movement and an association of well-known climate scientists, sufficiency (appropriate living standards) as a climate protection measure has become a topic of public discussion. Two years later, some governments issue longer warranty periods as well as advertising bans.

In the fall, schoolchildren and teachers around the world organize strike months during which they focus their learning on whatever they are interested in.

Housing markets collapse in Europe and North America due to speculation and falling rents. Numerous buildings are taken over by squatters, people resist evictions and establish housing councils. Many flats are transferred to the public sector, cooperatives and neighborhoods.

The wall between Mexico and the US is finally completed – by which time it has already been breached in dozens of places by refugees.

The "public money – public good" campaign becomes EU law: proprietary software is banned in public institutions and open-source software is promoted.

Fridays for Future, Extinction Rebellion and Ende Gelände join forces in Europe to launch a widespread civil disobedience campaign against fossil fuel infrastructure and for a different future for coal workers.

The government in Tunisia, newly elected after massive protests, introduces a visa fee of €250 for EU citizens to put pressure on the opening of the EU border.

The former coal mining areas in Germany join forces to form the "Good Life" test region and insist on democratizing their region by introducing citizens' forums.

The first Europe-wide feminist-migrant strike in the care sector demands better working conditions and pay, triggering a social debate.

2025

Energy & Climate

Education

Housing

Freedom of Movement

Technology

Energy & Climate

Freedom of Movement

2026

Energy & Climate

Employment

2026

Education

Teachers in Canada and Central Europe shorten the school timetable. They teach for only three hours a week and for the rest of the time provide support for the school pupils' projects.

Food & Agriculture

The film Anukta and Simon – Food Superheroes, which is about two farmers and their fight for socio-ecological agriculture, becomes a global success with more than 500 million viewers.

Housing

Communal living spaces are booming in the US corn belt as more and more people move to live and work in the countryside.

Finance

The "By 2025 We Rise Up" alliance blocks the New York and Tokyo stock exchanges for a week to show that systemic change is the only way out of the climate catastrophe.

Technology

The 1000th Open Workshop is opened in the UK, where people can tinker, build and repair things by themselves.

Food & Agriculture

Cooperatively run grocers and solidarity-based agriculture are on the rise worldwide, and the trend towards supermarkets is being reversed.

2027

Mobility & Transport

Massive protests during the holidays block air- and seaports in Canada. Remarkably, the demonstrators include many conservative politicians who have reconsidered their position due to the obligations they feel towards their grandchildren.

Housing

The right to housing is enshrined in law in Denmark, Norway and some US states: from now on, no one is homeless in these countries, everyone who stays in one of these countries for a longer period of time has the right to housing.

Food & Agriculture

Factory farming is banned in France, followed within six years by the rest of the EU as well as China and the US. Brazil ends soybean cultivation on former rainforest land.

Freedom of Movement

More than 1,000 cities around the world have declared themselves "safe havens." They have their own ships and use them to save the lives of thousands of migrants.

Global redistribution

▶ One of the key megatrends between the 2020s and 2048 was that the world became more just. Whereas the distribution of wealth, resources, power, prosperity and opportunities was still extremely unequal in 2024, by 2048 it had roughly equalized in all dimensions, both within societies and globally between different regions and continents.

The processes of redistribution and re-appropriation that led to this situation were neither linear nor free of conflicts; there were setbacks and intense debates. This trend toward increasing equality was driven mainly by social movements from the Global South that came together under the slogan "Payback time!" and increasingly networked and questioned the global distribution of power and resources. They worked closely with anti-racist and (climate) justice movements from the Global North that criticized racism, capitalist competition, and the imperial mode of living. A strengthened international, solidarity-based trade union movement focused on working conditions in the Global South and ensured that international legal regulations were tightened. The union movement particularly concentrated their direct actions and campaigns on exploitative transnational corporations. At the same time, people began raising awareness about and criticizing (neo) colonial exploitation, environmental destruction, and human rights violations, which had previously been considered essential yet invisible preconditions of "prosperity."

In many countries in the former Global South, the growing decolonialization movements brought governments to power that suspended unfair global trade agreements and demanded global freedom of movement. In close cooperation, this coalition replaced the global hegemonic power of the West. However, instead of acting with impunity as new superpowers, they focused on developing a →

→ form of global policy that was based on solidarity, deepening global democracy, fair international trade, and a fundamental peace. After a sharp increase in the early 2020s, the numbers of wars and armed conflicts dropped, and most weapons were done away with as a result of disarmament agreements and production bans until 2048.

Borders were gradually opened. This occurred because people simply used their right to freedom of movement. They were supported at first by networks of solidarity cities that housed them, and this situation was formally institutionalized in treaties in the late 2020s.

Radical polices of redistribution began to be put in place all over the world. These included socio-ecological tax reforms, property taxes and high taxes on inheritances. A wide-ranging series of debt cuts and debt relief programs – first and foremost in the Global South – were also key. At the same time, waves of appropriation took place – particularly during crises – in which staff took over companies, farmers appropriated the land that they worked, and people occupied living spaces. The original owners did attempt to overturn these actions in the courts, but eventually accepted the new circumstances – sometimes after mediation by locally recognized authorities and the provision of appropriate compensation. Reconciliation commissions were set up in many places, and progressive governments that wanted to implement greater equality provided the legal foundations to do so. Reparations for the Global South for centuries of colonial and climate debt were negotiated: these included finance, transfers of means of production, access to knowledge and technologies and formal apologies. These redistribution measures and processes of appropriation facilitated the continuous expansion of social security provisions worldwide.

The new eco-social government in the US transfers the large digital corporations Amazon, Apple, Google and Meta into public democratic ownership and divides them into smaller companies; at the same time, divestment leads to the withdrawal of money from similarly harmful start-ups in Silicon Valley.

The three-year #DefundFrontex campaign has seen funding for the European Border and Coast Guard Agency cut further and further. At the end of the year, the organization is completely dissolved.

The Union for Justice is founded as a coalition of 45 African and South American unions. In the years that follow, it plays a key role in the fight for better working conditions in the Global South.

The open-source video conferencing platform V_Conf calculates that around 300,000 tons of CO2 were saved through people using its video conferences instead of taking business trips.

School pupils occupy arms factories and defense ministries in Portugal, Poland and Indonesia and ultimately lead the military budget to be halved and redistributed to the education sector.

Christchurch, New Zealand; Cork, Ireland; Bergen, Norway; and Hamburg, Germany celebrate car-free weekends. YouTubers report enthusiastically from the streets.

The University of Mannheim is the 25th university in German-speaking countries to replace the study of traditional economics with that of plural economics.

To equalize living conditions, neglected residential areas around the world have their rents reduced or frozen before the buildings undergo environmental conversion in line with residents' needs. Living space in wealthy neighborhoods that is not used or underused is being redistributed.

Workers in 23 US states as well as Canada have the right to sabbaticals, which means they can take longer breaks from work without losing their job.

2028

Technology

Freedom of Movement

Democracy

Energy & Climate

Education

Mobility & Transport

Economy

Housing

Employment

Food & Agriculture

The European agricultural policy is completely switched to the promotion of organic and regional agriculture, with a focus on smallholders. Food produced in Europe can be exported only in exceptional cases, so that local markets elsewhere are no longer negatively affected.

Mobility & Transport

Mercedes-Benz lays off half of its employees for operational reasons. All employees are covered by the state transformation fund. Due to the general reduction in working hours, everyone finds a new job, many transition to the care sector.

Employment

Care councils are springing up in numerous cities and organizing local care structures. Outpatient care is therefore now available in many local districts.

Finance

The financial crash was used politically to socialize or wind down big banks, separate commercial and investment banks, introduce a financial transaction tax and ban derivatives.

Freedom of Movement

Several EU members declare sea rescue a national responsibility. Some EU member states are being sued and held accountable for their border policies over the past few decades.

Technology

Public money is available only for the development of open access commons and charitable or cooperative organizations.

Freedom of Movement

The three-year #DefundFrontex campaign has seen funding for the European Border and Coast Guard Agency cut further and further. At the end of the year, the organization is completely dissolved.

2029

Energy & Climate

Massive protests disrupt climate negotiations in Budapest so completely that they are moved to Johannesburg – but massive protests take place there too, and the negotiations are broken off entirely. Over the next few years, the Global Council for Sustainability emerges from the debate between science, politics and social movements.

Education

In Catalonia, Houses of Learning replace the current school model and serve as an example for the educational landscape of the future.

Environmental transformation

▶ Faced with accelerating environmental breakdown, the decline of destructive practices were particularly sharp during the late 2020s. Resource consumption was severely curtailed, and the pressure on ecosystems from greenhouse gases as well as chemical and other pollutants was drastically reduced. Starting in the 2030s, animal and plant biodiversity increased again in many areas – renaturation, environmentally-conscious utilization and the designation of nature reserves by the local population played important roles in this trend. Completely new approaches to agriculture and urban planning were developed – labels for products from organic farming disappeared because pesticide-free agriculture that no longer uses fossil-based fertilizers became the new standard. New and rediscovered forms of cultivation increased soil fertility. Urban green areas were redesigned as habitats and edible landscapes. As a result, people's relationship with nature changed fundamentally: society came to realize that it was part of the natural world and that humans need to live in fruitful co-existence with all of life of the planet instead of exploiting it.

The foundations for many of these developments were laid in 2025, when a broad transnational climate justice movement resurfaced, much bigger than in the late 2010s, and exerted its influence through disruptive school strikes, direct actions and targeted political campaigns. This led many people to view the climate catastrophe as an important issue not least because of the catastrophic changes that were already noticeable, such as unprecedented hot, dry summers and extreme weather events. Farmers' associations also recognized the problem and changed their lobbying strategy. At first, they turned to violent protests against all sorts of environmental policies. Realizing then that farming formed an integral part of the social-ecological transformation, they put forward very concrete solutions to save their future and those of societies to come. One important →

turn was a new set-up of agricultural subsidies. Instead of supporting industrial and large-scale agricultural companies, subsidies were re-designed to serve small-scale ecological farming. In many places, experiments in eco-friendly management and living flourished. Once they were embedded within with a favorable tax framework, more and more people got involved. Ultimately, the advocates of environmentally destructive practices – and above all, the fossil fuel energy companies and the automobile industry – lost much of their popular support and political power.

During this time, various social movements and more and more political parties were calling for transformative social and environmental measures. They recognized that advocates of the non-human environment and social justice movements could no longer be played off against one another. Alliances of environmental, climate, anti-racism, food sovereignty groups, LGBTQIA+ networks, trade unions and many others demanded not only car-free inner cities and an end to fossil fuels, but also socially just transitions to new livelihoods for the workers of the fossil fuel and automotive industries. Furthermore, they extended their demands to the entire social and employment system. Concepts of just transition, developed by local transformation councils, were put in place in every region.

Social security provisions and a redistribution of labor meant that it was finally possible to implement environmental policies that had long been sacrificed to the goals of economic growth, full employment and national competitiveness. This included protecting large spaces of nature, the sharp and then complete reduction of fossil fuels for production and alignment of industrial policies with the 1.5-degree limit. The result was a sustainable economy that had moved away from resource-intensive manufacturing and towards a truly circular economy, organic agriculture and fair distribution. In many places, this had already been achieved by the early 2030s.

5,000 wheelchair users and senior citizens block a major crossroads in Berlin, while 3,000 more block the roundabout around the Arc de Triomphe in Paris. They demand greater self-determination and autonomy in care as well as an end to poverty among the elderly.

An international pact for sustainable investments, put underway by massive pressure from the Global Food Council, brings about an end to land-grabbing, the return of land to local populations and compensation payments. Around the world, the trend towards rural exodus is being reversed as people are provided with an opportunity to cultivate land.

We'll Come United demonstrations take place in all major European cities at the same time – more than one million people come together in Rome.

The governments in Europe and the US incorporate large-scale companies, including large real estate groups and energy suppliers. Their profits and reserves are used to mitigate environmental damage and support those regions that have already suffered greatly from climate change.

2030

The network of solidarity cities includes more than half of all major cities in Europe and North Africa.

A global civil society campaign for reparations instead of debt culminates in a four-day blockade of the International Monetary Fund's annual meeting. In the coming months, 80% of all international debt is canceled and a comprehensive program to offset climate debt and colonial inequality is agreed on.

Healthy eating, farming and food processing are becoming a core learning focus in Spain's Houses of Learning.

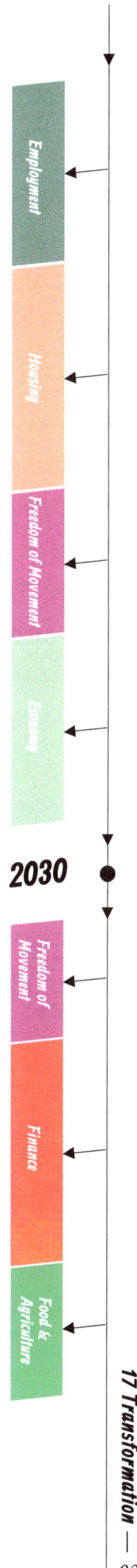

Employment

Housing

Freedom of Movement

Economy

Freedom of Movement

Finance

Food & Agriculture

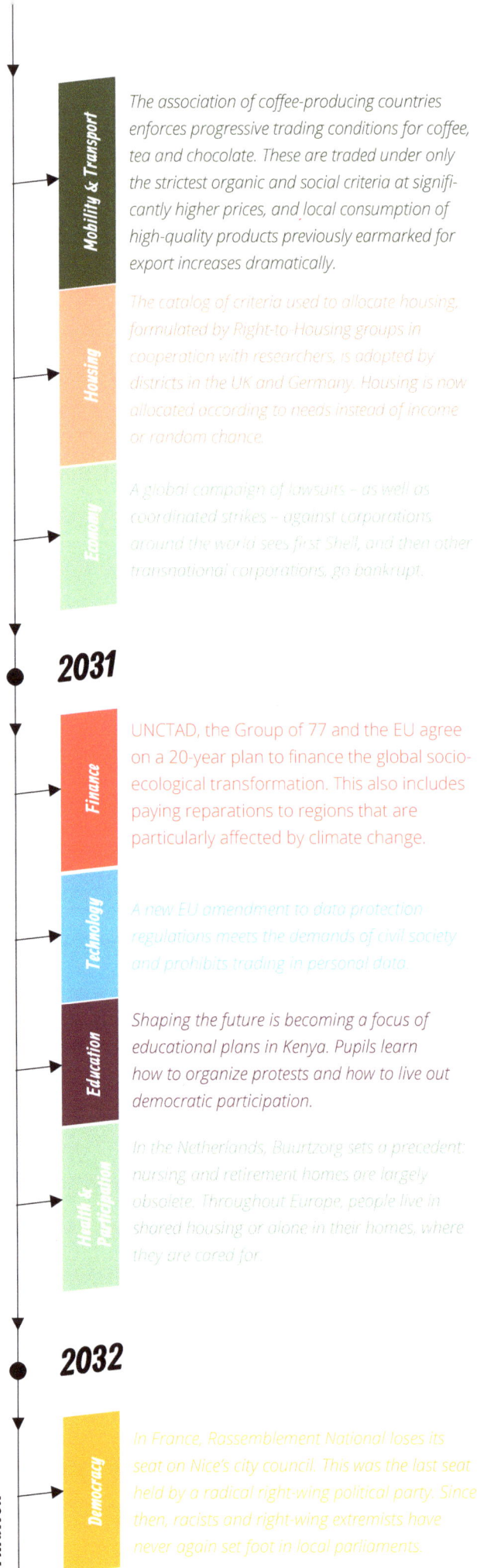

Mobility & Transport

The association of coffee-producing countries enforces progressive trading conditions for coffee, tea and chocolate. These are traded under only the strictest organic and social criteria at significantly higher prices, and local consumption of high-quality products previously earmarked for export increases dramatically.

Housing

The catalog of criteria used to allocate housing, formulated by Right-to-Housing groups in cooperation with researchers, is adopted by districts in the UK and Germany. Housing is now allocated according to needs instead of income or random chance.

Economy

A global campaign of lawsuits – as well as coordinated strikes – against corporations around the world sees first Shell, and then other transnational corporations, go bankrupt.

2031

Finance

UNCTAD, the Group of 77 and the EU agree on a 20-year plan to finance the global socio-ecological transformation. This also includes paying reparations to regions that are particularly affected by climate change.

Technology

A new EU amendment to data protection regulations meets the demands of civil society and prohibits trading in personal data.

Education

Shaping the future is becoming a focus of educational plans in Kenya. Pupils learn how to organize protests and how to live out democratic participation.

Health & Participation

In the Netherlands, Buurtzorg sets a precedent: nursing and retirement homes are largely obsolete. Throughout Europe, people live in shared housing or alone in their homes, where they are cared for.

2032

Democracy

In France, Rassemblement National loses its seat on Nice's city council. This was the last seat held by a radical right-wing political party. Since then, racists and right-wing extremists have never again set foot in local parliaments.

Transformation of the economy

▶ Between 2024 and 2048, the entire economy – that is, the production and distribution of goods and services – was fundamentally transformed, democratized and realigned. The democratization of the economy not only changed the role of the markets, but also redefined the fundamentals of business. Satisfying people's needs without living at the expense of others was to become a central aspect of today's society.

At its core, this transformation consisted of three parallel developments that have yet to be completed. First, the dominance of markets and the market logic was continuously pushed back. Markets now exist only in areas where the people have decided that they still make sense. Political regulation and democratic operation are used to ensure that the remaining markets are geared towards meeting people's needs and the common good. Second, more and more areas that are necessary for a good life and participation in society were organized as essential public services and made accessible to all. This socialization was different from former nationalizations of utility providers: it put people in charge and established real democratic ownership and management. Third, more and more self-run alternatives emerged that implemented the principles of a solidarity-based gift economy without market principles; people produce for the community and are provided for by it. ▶ 3 Economy

Over time, the emphasis shifted toward self-run commons and away from markets – a trend that accelerated beginning in the 2030s. A fundamental change in ownership was central to all three developments, so that by the beginning of the 2040s, all important means of production and larger assets were socialized. Today, these are managed democratically by municipalities, cities, cooperatives, and other council-based democratic bodies together with local citizens; this enables the economy to be run by everyone, for everyone.

The global economic crisis triggered by a financial crash that burst the "carbon bubble" of the fossil →

fuel industry in 2028 was an important turning point. Market and free trade-oriented economics, which had dominated debates and politics, was turned on its head. People began to understand that markets only make sense if they serve people's needs and protect the environment. If not, then a sector was to be organized cooperatively.

Social movements pressured governments to combine economic rescue measures with fundamental economic restructuring. The feminist and migrant strikes in the supply-related sectors of care, retail and gastronomy achieved equal pay and better working conditions. This also heralded intense debates, disputes and the end of the sexist and racist division of labor. People began criticizing the obligation to work for wages and the dependence on growth. This led to a radical reduction in working hours and to the expansion of public services. To buffer the effects of the financial crash, some countries in Europe introduced a basic income that ensured people could fully participate in society; they were followed by other large economies as the crisis worsened. Working hours were further reduced due to pressure from staff who were supported by the trade unions. Starting at the end of the 2020s, the 28-hour week became the new standard, with no wage reduction for the lower tariff groups. It has now been further reduced to 20 hours per week.

All banks and insurance companies – as well as businesses that depended on state subsidies – were either fully incorporated into public ownership or else had to implement strong criteria that ensured that they would work for the common good. Many companies facing bankruptcy were taken over by staff and have continued as cooperatives. Targeted infrastructure loans for cooperative companies led to the rapid spread of the solidarity-based economy in regional cycles. Local supply communities made the exit from the market ever easier. More and more people discovered the ease and value of cooperation as well as meaningful, self-determined activity in sustainable more regional economic circulation.

Boycotts and direct action against airlines that conduct deportations build up so much pressure that they abandon all deportations. Instead, solidary transport companies are emerging that specialize in expanding the legal scope for safe transport routes – including by plane.

Freedom of Movement

A general raw-materials strike takes place that is supported first by the African Union and then by other countries in the Global South. The strike results in a global democratic agreement stipulating the need for a circular economy and fair raw material trading.

Global Justice

Under pressure from the new coalition of countries of the Global South together with China and Brazil, the International Monetary Fund is democratized and a clearing union is introduced with a true international currency: Bancor 2.0.

Finance

2033

In Australia, public transport and public buildings are made 100% accessible for the disabled, as are at least 83% of all new flats.

Health & Participation

A networking conference of 20,000 initiatives from all over the world is held in Porto Alegre, Brazil. The groups have extended the principles of solidarity agriculture to other areas including supraregional trade.

Global Justice

In Ireland, half of all local authorities have taken back ownership and control of their energy and water supplies.

Energy & Climate

New education plans are ceremoniously passed in the US, where schools, pressure to perform and grades are abolished.

Education

2034

One thousand European cities allocate new living space solely in line with needs and no longer according to price.

Housing

The International Criminal Court begins prosecuting ecocide and other environmental crimes.

Energy & Climate

Holiday sailing ships have replaced fossil-fuel-driven cruise ships in Europe as the most popular form of travel.

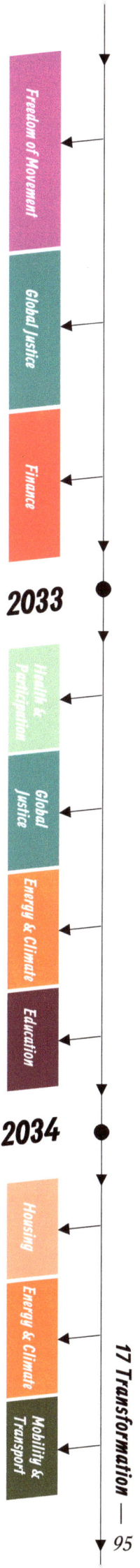

Mobility & Transport

2035

Food & Agriculture
Industrial mass fisheries in Europe are converted to small-scale fisheries in European waters. African fishers receive support to rebuild their local fisheries. An international moratorium on overfishing is passed.

Mobility & Transport
The 1000th village shop is opened in Salir, Portugal. The Village Shop Initiative has thus met its target.

Economy
Global negotiations on disarmament lead to a ban on the manufacture of automatic weapons.

Energy & Climate
Two-thirds of developed countries report that they have met their targets on reducing greenhouse gas emissions by 95%.

Freedom of Movement
An EU law amendment legalizes the situation of everyone on EU territory. Deportation camps are abolished, and comprehensive and equal participation opportunities are provided for everyone – including undocumented citizens.

2036

Mobility & Transport
80% of European workers now commute to work by bike.

Food & Agriculture
The Council for the Future recommends separating feces and urine when building and converting sewage systems worldwide and also using human feces for compost. Public health movements adapt the motto of the climate justice movement to "Shut shit down."

2037

Housing
After a referendum, a new EU directive transfers all land into communal ownership and outlaws its privatization.

Democracy
After two years of negotiations, the Constitutional Convention of the US adopts a new constitution. Its most important goal is ensuring that everyone can participate in all decisions that affect their lives.

Employment
The World Bank completes its restructuring process. 50% of World Bank positions are filled by women, 80% by black, indigenous, and people of color.

Dismantling discrimination and domination

From the mid-2020s onward, society increasingly began to question, combat and dismantle all forms of discrimination and domination. As difficult as this process was, the goal was simple: no one should be disadvantaged or privileged. Racism, sexism, classism, and discrimination against against homosexuals and transpersons, the elderly, children and people with physical or mental disabilities, as well as all other forms of discrimination were actively countered by strong societal forces.

The aim was to redistribute economic, social, ideological, personal, legal and political power: numerous laws were redrawn in the 2020s and 30s. Backlash in the early 2020s only showed how discrimination benefited some at the expense of others and that the influence of the former had to be broken. In addition to gender mainstreaming, ways of examining the law with regards to other forms of discrimination were developed. Quotas led to a fundamental change in the labor market. Exclusion, sexual harassment and other everyday forms of discrimination were recognized early on by more and more people, who learned to oppose them resolutely in everyday life – both privately and publicly. Racist statues and street names were replaced, non-binary gender roles were taken into account in all official documents, and language that discriminated against people with impairments disappeared – this is how norms and values changed.

The impetus behind the fundamental changes that took place in all areas of society came from very different directions, but they were linked to one another in solidarity: the Black Lives Matter and Defund the Police movements addressed racist police violence and laws, anti-racist alliances focused on everyday racism, self-run refugee and post-migrant groups supported refugees and broad coalitions collaborated in the fierce struggles against the fascist right; queer–feminist movements targeted discrimination based on sexual orientation and gender identity, the care movement criticized the exploitation of migrant caregivers, and trade unions focused on class-based discrimination. →

On a personal level, these fundamental changes led to privileged people recognizing their position in society, reflecting on it and working to reduce discrimination – and in doing so, they shared a lot of power. Self-reflection groups (e.g. on critical masculinity and critical whiteness) played a strong role in this process, as did discussions and joint debates about discrimination in organizations and in the workplace. Intersectional empowerment groups became a common feature in many places, strengthening and accelerating the transformations.

The changes that took place at the personal level also had an impact on discourses – sexist advertising, all-male panels, exclusive white organizations, and public buildings without lifts all began to seem increasingly outdated. Instead, unisex toilets and anti-discrimination training became the norm, with freedom of movement becoming recognized as a human right.

Not everyone supported the complex process of dismantling social discrimination and domination – some people tried to hold on to their privileges and defended them in everyday life through exclusionary politics. But these positions have since been marginalized and right-wing parties are now isolated. This came about through decisive intervention and solidarity, and because the people who wanted to live in a world where everyone was entitled to full participation stood together.

Over time, the perceived differences between people, which had been constructed over centuries, became less important – and with them the impacts of racism, sexism, classism and other forms of domination were likewise banished. A person's heritage, what they looked like, their parents' or grandparents' professions, their beliefs, and how closely they corresponded to (earlier) norms of body and performance began to have less and less impact on everyday lives, opportunities and participation in society. Gender hardly plays a role at all now, and gender boundaries have become fluid. People can be who they are and love who they want without being judged – and without suffering social or economic consequences.

Much of this progress has been made possible by changes to the economic and democratic systems – in particular, the reduction in working hours changed the division of labor between all genders, social security provisions reduced fears of downward social mobility, and broader participation helped counteract exclusion.

2038

Finance

The last private pension insurance in the UK is dissolved because the basic income has made it obsolete. The remaining funds are transferred to the "Boomers for Justice" reparations fund, which was set up for this purpose in 2027. The fund builds infrastructure in the Global South to help deal with the consequences of the climate catastrophe.

2039

Global Justice

Split, Croatia, and Teyateyaneng, Lesotho, ratify the 250th South–North municipal partnership. The aim of such partnerships is to share experiences about socio-ecological lifestyles.

Mobility & Transport

Michigan Central Station, reopened in 2030, has been voted the most beautiful train station in the world. Among other distinguishing features, it has an impressive waiting area with a music room, a solar-powered sauna and a ball pit for children made from renewable raw materials.

2040

Employment

Across Europe, 50% of companies (amounting to 76% of employees) are organized as cooperatives, and the trend is rising.

2041

Housing

In Stratford, England, the last tenement house is saved from demolition and reopened as the Museum of Unjust Housing.

2042

Technology

90% of the world's population own a resource-saving and energy efficient mobile device.

Freedom of Movement

The external borders of the EU are opened to everyone; all entry restrictions are dropped. In terms of freedom of movement, the EU is thus catching up with the African Union, which already did so in 2033.

2043

Economy

The Federation of Commoning Municipalities celebrates an important milestone: 500 municipalities of various sizes are now operating completely without income and in line with the principle of contribution instead of exchange.

2044

Technology

Nuclear fusion researchers announces that the technology will likely become available within the next 30 years.

2045

Energy & Climate

A new United Nations report shows that global biodiversity has once again increased slightly over the past decade due to the expansion of forest and wildlife areas carefully managed by local residents.

2046

Manufacturing & Companies

Worldwide, 98.34% of all non-renewable raw materials are being recycled. A global agreement regulates the flow of materials and develops requirements for their processing and separability.

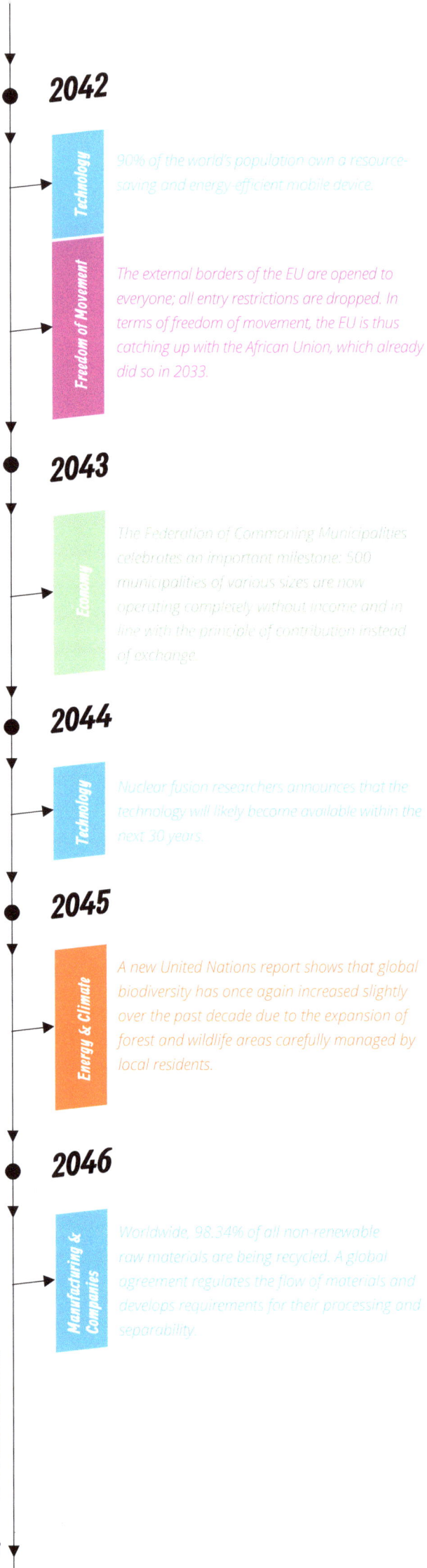

Self-determination and democratization

▶ Since the 2020s, society has become increasingly democratic – self-determination at all levels and in all areas of society was the driving force behind all the trends outlined above.

Democratization led to the redistribution of power – from centralized governments and parliaments to regions, municipalities, cities, communities, and neighborhoods; from major shareholders and boards to workers' councils, cooperatives and collectives; from the few to the many.

Democratization took hold because people were rightly outraged that demands – even those based on strong democratic majorities – were still not being implemented. Exemplary were the demands for climate protection, global justice, decolonization, and peace, which were backed by powerful movements and strong transnational majorities. Because they had strong public support, yet their demands were not translated into policy by the late 2020s, people began to found initiatives, climate and future councils, solidarity cities and political parties, and launched a variety of other democratic experiments. The aim was to implement their demands and to organize and appropriate the means to do so in order to take the necessary change towards climate justice, peace and solidarity at the local level.

The solidarity-based self-help networks that sprung up everywhere led to the development of neighborhood structures in many places that provided people with food and offered spaces to meet at a time when many people felt isolated and alone. These early forms of today's Community Centers were at the core of democratization (▶ 11 Housing). In the 2020s, more and more cities rebelled, following Barcelona's example. The governments of these cities and city groups gradually began to hand over power to local bodies.

In addition to these urban experiments, strong processes of democratization also took place in the countryside. Regions such as the anti-nuclear region in Wendland, Germany, the Zone à Defendre →

Employment

2048

Democracy

Due to the elimination of inequality and discrimination, there has been no war in the world for 10 years. This is celebrated around the world in August as "Mês de Alegria" (the Month of Joy).

→ (ZAD) in France, or cooperation Jackson in Jackson, Mississippi were based on the structures also found in Chiapas and Rojava and became models for council-based democratic organizing.

Greater social equality as well as more opportunities for co-determination and participation made such experiments and places where democracy was practiced increasingly popular. As a result, national and state governments, as well as city and local councils, were compelled to officially recognize more and more of these experiments.

For their part, small and medium-sized companies could no longer evade the support for co-determination and participation, and were transformed into cooperatives or collectives run by their staff. Large companies listed on the stock exchange remained the last refuge of hierarchical structures for a long time. However, they were eventually transformed into democratic corporate forms through participatory decision-making and broken up into smaller units.

*All of the currents of societal transformation were interlinked and reinforcing one another. **A future for all** was established through the joint effort of many different people. We sketch some of the events that could have taken place along the way in the timeline on the last pages. We hope that our narrative and the events described make a systemic transformation of society conceivable. Whether it is also possible depends on all of us.*

How did this vision come about?

This vision was drawn up between 2019 and 2022 through collaboration between the grassroots think and do tank **Konzeptwerk Neue Ökonomie** (Laboratory for New Economic Ideas) in Leipzig, Germany, and many partners. The project was inspired by two questions: *What type of society would we like to live in?* and *What can we do to create that society?* We could not – nor did we want to – try to answer these questions by ourselves, which is why we devised Future Workshops to develop specific ideas with people from civil society who were experts in different topics. These people either run practical projects, are part of social movements or organizations, or conduct academic research.

The method:
Future Workshops

The core ideas behind our vision of a **Future for All** emerged from twelve Future Workshops undertaken in 2019. Twelve to twenty pioneers came together for two days to think, develop visions, and discuss them intensively. In order to ensure that we covered a broad range of positions at each workshop, we divided the topics among the four authors and prepared each area with one or two external partners (▸ Acknowledgements). This enabled us to identify the core issues of each topic beforehand and come up with a relevant list of people to invite. The partners also provided advice during preparation and follow-up.

We developed the workshops using Robert Jungk's concept of "Future Workshops." Each was carried out in the same manner during one or two days. The workshops took place in three consecutive phases: critique, utopia and strategy. We shortened the first phase by collecting critiques in the respective area of society in advance with a questionnaire and then presenting, supplementing and discussing the answers we received. The utopia and strategy phases lasted for 1.5 hours each and involved small groups discussing different fields. We collected ideas on cards, which were later sorted and discussed together. These were then presented to the other participants in 'gallery tours,' after which they were discussed and prioritized. The critique and utopia phases took place on the first day; the second day was allocated to the strategy phase. This ensured that the participants could share an evening meal together and that there would be ample time between the considerations.

The Future Workshops led to intensive discussions, which, in turn, produced jointly weighted collections of cards. The cards were photographed, typed up and shared with all participants in text form.

Building on these results, the four-person team of authors discussed, structured and wrote for several months. We consulted with the partners of the workshops, sought advice from experts on various topics and reflected on the content with friends and colleagues. The texts were also revised by four professional proofreaders.

Who was involved?

Even though the vision of the future for all was developed by people who currently live in German-speaking countries, it is based on a global justice perspective. This perspective was central in all the Future Workshops. During some workshops, this perspective was especially prominent, particularly when addressing the issues of global trade and South–North relations, financial systems, energy/climate and freedom of movement.

Our goal for the workshops was to include a broad section of society and for the participants to come from different backgrounds. We succeeded in bringing together actors with diverse positions from within the emancipatory spectrum. This was also noted by the participants themselves and recognized as progress compared to many other workshops.

However, we were not able to achieve the same level of diversity in terms of privileges and social positions – even though we tried to do so. In all Future Workshops, participants with different social positions took part. Nevertheless, people who tend to be discriminated against (apart from cis women) were always in the minority, except for the workshop on freedom of movement. Overall, about half of the participants were women and half were men. Inter-, transgender, non-binary as well as queer people, people with impairments, people without higher educational attainment, and people who are racially discriminated against were not sufficiently present. The reasons for this are manifold and relate not only to the work of the Konzeptwerk, but also to power relations in general.

In terms of the specific project, we did not have enough time or resources to highlight a variety of viewpoints and perspectives. Therefore, Konzeptwerk runs a strategy to diversify, which has led to significant changes in the organization by 2024.

What are the authors' positions in society?

As authors, we are aware of our own social positions as well. We are all white, cisgender and living in heterosexual partnerships; half of us are male, the other half female; none of us have impairments and all have been to university. We grew up in East and South Germany and now live in Leipzig, Halle and Berlin. There are differences among the economic situations of our families of origin, but all belong to the middle class. We are thus similarly positioned and privileged, which means that our team does not reflect the diversity in society or the distribution of power. This further means that our perspectives run the risk of reproducing particular power relations since everyone's position in society determines their point of view and inevitably limits them. We have long dealt with privilege and discrimination, both personally and in our collectives. It is imperative that we change the social balance of power – both small- and large-scale – and we hope we are on the right track.

We sought to include different views in the Future for All project by jointly developing the content during future workshops. As described above, our approach had its limits, but around 200 people were involved in the development process. We believe that this is reflected in the texts. Finally, we welcome any and all feedback and critique.

More on Konzeptwerk Neue Ökonomie: ▸ **konzeptwerk-neue-oekonomie.org/english/**

Acknowledgements

We would like to thank everyone who has contributed to this vision, in particular:

⬡ *Andrea Vetter* (project support, advice and editing), *Mona Hofmann* (co-organized the future workshops), *Josefa Kny* and *Eva Mahnke* (editing), *Diana Neumerkel* (typesetting and layout), *Manuel Schroeder* (illustrations), *Hannes Lindenberg* (website), *Simon Phillips* (English translation) as well as *Divij Kapur* and *Emily Pickerill* (English proofreading). For the English edition, *Steffen Böhm* (contact to Mayfly), and *Jess Parker* (layout) from Mayfly.

⬡ We are also very grateful to our contacts at the funding organizations that supported the project financially.
→ *Friedrich-Ebert-Stiftung*:
Manuela Matthess, Christiane Heun, Sarah Ganter, Frederike Boll und Katharina Lepper.
→ *Rosa-Luxemburg-Stiftung*:
Steffen Kühne and Adriana Yee Mayberg.
→ *Heinrich-Böll-Stiftung*:
Linda Schneider, Lili Fuhr and Christine Chemnitz.

⬡ We would also like to thank everyone who was involved in devising and organizing the future workshops and writing the texts:
Alessa Hartmann, Alexis Passadakis, Anja Wiesental, Bettina Müller, Charlotte Hitzfelder, Jana Gebauer, Janna Aljets, Jona Blum, Julianna Fehlinger, Lina Hurlin, Marc Amann, Margret Rasfeld, Max Frauenlob, Miriam Gutekunst, Nicolas Guenot, Otto Herz, Riadh Ben Ammar, Ronald Blaschke, Ronja Morgenthaler, Sven Drebes, Tilman Santarius, Werner Rätz.

⬡ We are also grateful to the more than *200 experts and pioneers* from social movements, research, and NGOs who participated in the future workshops and therefore significantly contributed to the development of the ideas behind this vision.

⬡ We would like to thank :
Alex Demirovic, Fabian Scheidler, Friederike Habermann, Simon Sutterlütti for discussing content and providing advice, and *Netzwerk Ökonomischer Wandel (NOW)* for joint reflection.

⬡ Thanks also goes to our colleagues from *Konzeptwerk* for the many years of working together on the ideas behind this vision, to *Clemens Herrmann* from oekom-Verlag for the German publication, and to the entire team at *MayFly books*.

⬡ Finally, we would like to express our gratitude to everyone who is not mentioned here by name but who has been involved in the past months and years.

Together we can make this vision a reality!

We are grateful for the financial support of the workshops
and publication by the following organisations:

FRIEDRICH EBERT STIFTUNG

ROSA LUXEMBURG STIFTUNG

Schöpflin Stiftung:

Future for all. A Vision for 2048
would not have been possible if not for the support and
cooperation of many people and organisations. Some of
those were:

Andreas Sallam

Anil Shah

Anne Bundschuh

NETZWERK Gerechter Welthandel

Anne Löscher

Wissenschaftliche Arbeitsgruppe Nachhaltiges Geld

Ann Wiesental

Netzwerk CARE REVOLUTION

Finanzwende

Dr. Christian Siefkes

Erik Albers

(Free Software Foundation Europe)

fsfe

Dr. Eva Wonneberger

(Via Institut)

Jan-Hendrik Cropp

UNDER COVER

Johannes Ostermeier

netzwerk n

Kashef

ALARM PHONE

Larisa Tsvetkova

NETZWERK IMMO VIEL IEN

Lotta De Carlo

Slow Food® Deutschland e.V.

Lucía Muriel

glokal

Ludwig Schuster

WECHANGE

Maja Volland

FORUM FAIRER HANDEL

Maren Kirchhoff

krit net

Margret Rasfeld

Schule im Aufbruch

Maria Hummel

NETZWERK FÜR DAS RECHT AUF
GESUNDHEITSVERSORGUNG
ALLER MIGRANT*INNEN

Mark Wege

einfach einsteigen

Otto Herz

Civil Courage
C
ausgezeichnet

Paavo Günther

HAVEL
🐱**i***

Rainer Rehak

FIfF
Forum
InformatikerInnen
für Frieden und
gesellschaftliche
Verantwortung

Rebecca Kleinheitz

ALLER WOHNEN eG

Regine Beyß

INTER KOMM

Ronald Blaschke

Netzwerk
Grundeinkommen

Sprecher*innenkreis

für eine
zukunftsfähige
Ernährungs- und Land-
wirtschaftspolitik
in der Region
Ernäh rungs rat BERLIN

Susanne Koch

schwarz wurzel
Biologisch · fair · kollektiv

Thomas Doennebrink

ouishare

Tina Röthig

Poliklinik Veddel

Tobi Rosswog

living *utopia*

Urs Mauk

URS MAUK
ReLaVisio

Viktoria Hellfeier

**W3 _ WERKSTATT
FÜR INTERNATIONALE
KULTUR UND POLITIK**

nyéléni .de
Wege zur
Ernährungssouveränität

Alfred Eibl,
Dagmar Paternoga,
Werner Rätz

attac

Dana Giesecke,
Josefa Kny,
Maxim Keller

FUTURZWEI
FUTURZWEI. STIFTUNG ZUKUNFTSFÄHIGKEIT

Johannes Schorling,
Lena Luig

INKOTA
netzwerk

Alessa Hartmann,
Bettina Müller,
Michael Reckordt

PowerShift

Ann-Kathrin Schneider (BUND) , Ariane Goetz (Uni Kassel), Barbara Sennholz-Weinhardt (Oxfam Deutschland e.V.), Bernd Sommer (Norbert Elias Center, Europa-Universität Flensburg), Bernhard Knierim (Bahn für Alle), Christoph Spahn, Dirk Posse, Efsun Kızılay (Rosa-Luxemburg- Stiftung), Elisabeth Voß (NETZ für Selbstverwaltung und Selbstorganisation), Friederike Habermann (Netzwerk Ökonomischer Wandel), Jana Gebauer (Die Wirtschaft der Anderen), Janine Korduan (TU Berlin und Heinrich-Böll-Stiftung), Julia Lingenfelder (Forum kritische politische Bildung), Julia Thrul, Karen Schewina, (Aktion Agrar e.V.), Katja Leyendecker (Changing Cities), Leonie Plänkers (FG Entwerfen und Städtebau, TU Darmstadt), Lina Hurlin (Mietshäuser Syndikat), Linda Schneider (Heinrich-Böll-Stiftung), Lisa Eberbach, Marc Amann (Neustart Tübingen), Marie Heitfeld (Germanwatch e.V.), Lars-Arvid Brischke (ifeu - Institut für Energie- und Umweltforschung), Lino Zeddies, Ruth Blanck, Sophia Tabea Salzberger (Fridays For Future), Sven Drebes, Timo Kaphengst (Regionalwert AG Berlin-Brandenburg), Tobias Haas, Tom Hansing (anstiftung), Vicky Eichhorn (Techgenossen eG), Werner Zingler (patient speaker in Berlin hospitals)

www.ingramcontent.com/pod-product-compliance
Lightning Source LLC
Chambersburg PA
CBHW051307270326
41927CB00023B/3473